A TWELVE STEP RECOVERY GUIDE AND WORKBOOK

~

A PATHWAY TO FREEDOM

Written By: A sober, grateful and repurposed alcoholic

Written For: Alcoholics and Victims of any addiction who are looking for a way out

Also of value to anyone else experiencing depression and or anxiety; regardless of causes or condition

Foresight Publishing (Canada)

1144 – 20 Fort St.
Winnipeg, Manitoba,
Canada   R3C 4L3
foresightpublishing@shaw.ca

Published: June, 2021
Edition: 14

This publication is in the public domain and may be freely copied or shared in whole or in part.

WORDS OF TRUTH
(*VERBUM VERITATIS*)

YOU ARE THE MANIFESTATION OF THE PROCESS OF CREATION: YOU BELONG HERE.

YOU ARE NOT AN ACCIDENT: THE ACT OF CREATION DOES NOT MAKE MISTAKES.

DESPITE HOW YOU MIGHT BE FEELING AT THIS MOMENT: YOU ARE SIGNIFICANT: YOU ARE SAFE AND YOU ARE SECURE.

WITHOUT ANY DOUBT, RIGHT NOW, YOU ARE EXACTLY WHERE YOU NEED TO BE: AND YOU ARE DOING PRECISELY WHAT YOU SHOULD BE DOING.

MOST IMPORTANTLY AND POSSIBLY DESPITE APPEARANCES; THE UNIVERSE IS CONTINUING TO UNFOLD AS IT SHOULD.

YOU'RE FUTURE BEGINS NOW – YOUR TRUE DESTINY IS WAITING.

(Anonymous)

DEDICATION

This workbook is dedicated to our sponsors and those that preceded them. They made up the chain of communication that brought the good news of recovery to those of us who are now attempting to share with others this priceless message of hope and healing. We also dedicate this thesis to the countless numbers of other recovering alcoholics who we have shared the 12 step road of happy destiny with over the years.

We say a heartfelt thank you not only to our sponsors, but to sponsors everywhere. You are the real glue that holds this life saving fellowship of ours together.

To you other alcoholics who shared the walk with us, we thank you as well. Not as much for what you had to say, but more for how you lived your life. By your actions, some of you have taught us what to do; and some of you have taught us what not to do. Both are of equal importance. May God continue to bless you all!

There are as many accounts of recovery as there are recovering alcoholics. In our case, we declare that we have neither discovered anything new ourselves nor have we figured out anything about recovery on our own. We tell you only what we have seen and heard and learned from others we have met through the course of our journey.

In simplest terms, we offer you this priceless and purposeful message of hope because the assurance for our own recovery demands that we actively practice the sharing of this *"good news"* with all who may be interested.

PREFACE

This workbook/guide is specifically designed to help you find your way through the twelve steps of recovery in an orderly, guided and productive manner. The twelve steps as described in the book Alcoholics Anonymous is not only a well proven recovery plan for alcoholics but are equally effective in addressing the needs of those suffering from any other addiction, whether it be chemical, psychological or behavior based.

As well; those suffering from many forms of depression and/or anxiety without the added complication of an addiction may find this approach beneficial because all addictions include the common symptoms of low self-esteem, personal inadequacy and a deep seated feeling of incompleteness. In fact, we suggest that anyone seeking escape from the excruciating pain associated with any disorder that includes a helpless and hopeless state of mind, body and spirit, regardless of the causes, can most certainly find help here.

As a starting point and also an important reminder, we suggest that you record your sobriety date on the first page of your personal copy of this workbook/guide. For you non alcoholics, your date of significance would be the date of the day that you first honestly reached out for help to address your specific problem(s). Finally, this process works equally well for anyone else that may be interested in finding a more satisfying and comfortable way of living.

Because what we describe here has been the single most influential and positive life altering experience we could ever possibly have hoped for and because we are convinced that this priceless gift can only be retained if we freely give it away; we are compelled to share this news with anyone who may be interested.

We encourage you to be of open mind and join us in this positively transformative and fascinating personal journey of *"uncovering, discovering, discarding and finally recovering"* from an otherwise hopeless condition of mind, body and spirit that is offered to us through our personal application of these 12 steps.

Although not conference approved, this guide is most definitely "AA" appropriate and does not in any way attempt to speak for or represent the fellowship of Alcoholics Anonymous. This workbook is simply an account of the experiences of a small group of alcoholics who have recovered from the disease of alcoholism; solely, wholly and only through applying the principles and practices of these twelve steps in the manner presented here in.

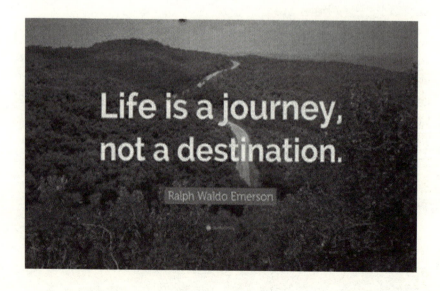

CONTENTS

Foreword — 11
Introduction — 17
Weekly Meeting Agenda — 19
Commitment Meeting — 20

Part 1: Finding Recovery
Steps One to Nine

Step One: 27
We admitted we were powerless over alcohol – that our lives had become unmanageable.

Mychal's Prayer — 29
Step 1: Worksheet — 31
A Native American Prayer — 35

Step Two: 36
We Came to believe that a power greater than ourselves could restore us to sanity.

Step 2: Worksheet — 39
The Mirror — 43

Step Three: 49

We made a decision to turn our will and our lives over to the care of God as we understood Him.

Step 3: Worksheet   50
Just for Today   54
Why Not Give It A Try   55
Some Timely and Priceless Suggestions   61

Steps Four and Five: 62
We made a searching and moral inventory of ourselves and
admitted to God, ourselves and another human being the exact nature of our wrongs.

Step 4: Worksheet   63
A Prayer of Surrender   67
My Personal Inventory   69
The Issue of Fear   71

Steps Six and Seven: 78
Were entirely ready to have God remove all of these defects of character.
We humbly asked Him to remove our shortcomings.

As I Think   81
Step 6&7: Worksheet   85
Will I Ever Get It?   91
The Search for Identity   96

Steps Eight and Nine   102
Made a list of all persons we had harmed and became willing to make amends to them all. We made direct

amends to such people wherever possible, except when to do so would injure them or others.

The Letter	103
Step 8&9: Worksheet	105
Recognizing Recovery	108
God's Grace	115

Part II: Growing In Recovery
Steps Ten to Twelve

Step Ten: 117
Continued to take personal inventory and when we were wrong, promptly admitted it.

Our True Home	120
My Medallion	124
Givers and Takers	125
This Day	130

Step Eleven: 131
We sought through prayer and meditation to improve our conscious contact with God as we understood Him, praying only for the knowledge of His will for us and the power to carry that out.

I am Resolved	135
Is this as Good as It is Ever Going to get?	138
Einstein: What I believe	143

Desired Things 148

Step Twelve: 149
Having had a spiritual awakening as the Result of these steps, we tried to carry the message to alcoholics and practice these principles in all our affairs.

Comments on Learning and Recovery 150
Living the Twelve Steps 153
A Member's Eye View of AA 158
Living with step one in recovery 161
Becoming A Spiritual Seeker 168
Fulfilling the Conditions for Recovery 187
A Universal Truth 190

Afterword

The Transition from Humanist to Spiritualist ... 193
The Elephant in the AA Meeting Room 196
The Key to a Full and Happy Life 201
Acknowledgements 205
Dare to Be 207
The Way It Is 208
Appendix 209

"The first step towards getting somewhere is to decide that you are not going to stay where you are."

~ J.P. Morgan

FOREWORD

One of humanity's most significant truths is that each of us knows that in many ways, we are all unique and quite different, one from another. We can thank the human faculty of *self-awareness* for this. As well and equally true; we are also very aware of being quite similar to one another in many other ways. At least in part, our mental health and wellbeing demands the establishment and maintenance of a dynamic and appropriate balance of these two contrasting perspectives in our psyche.

The question we want to ask ourselves is: Overall, do we perceive our self to be more different from those around us or are we more similar? Concerning those of us suffering from untreated addictions and/or clinical depression and low self-esteem, the truth is, we have lost touch with that balance of these contrasting perspectives - if in fact we ever had it.

Our experience was that for far too often, we found ourselves trapped in a very unhealthy and totally introverted psycho-somatic reality of being separate from and unhealthily different from those around us. The sad truth is, we were powerless to do anything about it.

The good news we bring to you today, is that even though we have individually travelled life's path separately, up to this point; there is most definitely a healing path forward that we can and should travel together. In itself, this common road to wellness can be a unifying and reconciling experience for all of us. Also, we need to know that our addictive behavior, whether it is chemical, psychological or behaviorally based is merely a symptom of a much deeper fundamental problem we all share with each other. You have been alone far too long.

Please join us now in the spirit of fellowship and singleness of purpose. For you non - alcoholics, feel free to substitute a personally more meaningful word or phrase describing your personal addiction or problem for the words *alcohol*, *alcoholic* or *alcoholis*m as you come across them in the text to follow. We are all suffering the same pain. Where we all come from may be different. However, the path forward is best travelled together.

In our particular situation and out of total desperation, we who write this missive ultimately were forced to do something we had previously vowed we would never do. We reached out for help and in less than 24 hours of so doing and full of fear and trepidation, we were escorted to the doors of Alcoholics Anonymous. We were instantly welcomed and accepted without question. In short order we were introduced to the oft-called *"AA-101"* or, if you prefer, the entry level advice for seeking sobriety. *"Don't drink! Go to meetings! Get a sponsor! Read the book!"* Fortunately for us having lost the will to fight, we capitulated. This simple action bought us a little time. The twelve steps and real recovery began a little later. That part of our story is the real focus of this book.

To prepare for the 12 steps, the first thing we had to learn is that as practicing alcoholics, we drank primarily to ease the pain of living and truthfully, it did help, at least in the beginning. Unfortunately, *"the cure"* itself became a problem of its own. The truth was, we had descended into the relentless and insidious trap of dependency and addiction and, in fact, had done so long before we realized it.

As practicing alcoholics, we are helplessly driven by an incessant craving to drink. It dominates our thinking. In order to overcome this craving, our recovery will demand the acquisition of a much more comfortable and satisfactory way of living in the absence of alcohol.

In the vast majority of cases this recovery process or *"psychic change"* as AA's first medical benefactor, Dr. William D. Silkworth labelled it, occurs as a process of small incremental changes over the course of time, in our attitudes, perceptions, assumptions and beliefs about life in general and our-selves in particular. This process of change is what the twelve steps of recovery is specifically designed to facilitate for those of us who are now too uncomfortable to stay where we are any longer and are willing to do something about it.

More specifically, the purpose of this guide is to help you identify clearly and unequivocally what your personal problem really is *(you may be pleasantly surprised with what you come to learn)*; and to then allow you to ask yourself at least some of the essential questions necessary in order to lead you towards recovery in a timely manner. At this point, you also need to know that you cannot acquire recovery like a new outfit. You already have it! You can only find true recovery within yourself.

<u>Please note</u>: To you the alcoholic reader, this book is not at all recommended to be used at any regular AA meetings or even at 12 step discussion meetings. The AA traditions advise us that those meetings must always focus on the primary source of direction as found in the first 164 pages of the Big Book and as well all other AA approved literature. To avoid possible dilution of the AA message we totally respect and support the AA policy of only using conference approved literature at AA meetings. AA must

remain diligent in preserving intact the priceless message of recovery as given to us by our pioneers.

This guide is meant solely as a supplement for any individual to use between meetings. In order to expand and enrich our personal growth, we as individuals seeking real recovery must always be free to access helpful resources outside of AA, just as our pioneers did in their own time and as described to us through their book titled *AA Comes of Age*.

Most certainly, not all of the questions that follow in the step worksheets, provided here in, are expected to be answered affirmatively, at least not in the beginning. They are designed primarily to help the sufferer get his/her thinking in the right place so that growth and healing can begin to take place.

Do not let any uncertainty about your answers to any of these questions keep you from forging ahead. You will hear over and over again in your journey here that **recovering is a process and not a destination.**

There will be challenges. Always remember that we are not perfect. It is the effort that counts; recovery starts on the inside and grows outward not the other way around. To simply keep trying is what successful recovery demands.

The suggestions and personal accounts addressing particular parts of the twelve steps found in this guide are experiences shared by ourselves, or are accounts directly related to us from other recovering alcoholics. Like everything else in this guide, they are meant to be suggestive only. Please take them or leave them as you see fit.

Also, the prayers, poetry and quotes included are those found to be most helpful to the authors in establishing and maintaining a positive and receptive state of mind. They are also only meant to be helpful and we invite you to also take them or leave them as you see fit.

Before we go any further in this guide, it is important to know that we assume the following to be true because this is how we continue to experience the reality of our own recovery. We believe that whole hearted acceptance of the following assumption is absolutely critical to finding our way to any meaningful recovery through this process.

"Concerning any venture we may engage in, we will be rewarded only in direct proportion to the energy and commitment we bring to the task. Recovery is most certainly a gift but does not just happen on its own. We have to work for it."

The good news is that in AA meetings all over the world today we will find individuals actively engaged in working the steps and applying the principles of good sober living in their daily lives. They are the members most often recognized by a welcoming friendly countenance, a quiet self-confidence and often are found to have a smile on their faces. These are the folks sometimes referred to as "the winners".

Unfortunately, we will also find those among us who have, by choice or simply by default, limited their investment in their own recovery to attending one or maybe two meetings a week, often without taking any direct participation, hoping only to absorb some recovery passively from others in the room. This group, believe it or not, also includes some who have been without drink for many years. These individuals are usually identifiable as the one's often exhibiting a frown on their face or at best a dour countenance and inevitably are complaining about one thing or another. They tend to sit apart and often are found looking at their shoes.

Both of these types and of course all others are equally welcome in the AA meeting rooms and we all exercise our right to participate any way we see fit. This is as it should be and must be. As we were in our own time, we encourage you to *"stick with the winners."* They have something to share with you of true value.

Finally, we wish that you experience the consciousness of God's presence in not only this exercise of applying the twelve steps but also for each and every day of the rest of your life.

When you hold resentment toward another, you are bound to that person or condition by an emotional link that is stronger than steel. Forgiveness is the only way to dissolve that link and regain your freedom.

~Katherine Ponder~

INTRODUCTION

What follows is an attempt to be proactive by trying to answer some timely questions that you, the reader, might want answered at this point, such as: Who are you? Why are you writing this book? What do you expect to accomplish? And maybe most importantly: What can you offer me that I do not already know?

To begin with, this treatise was written not to change anyone's mind. Instead, our purpose here is simply to reach out to those that already share a common vision with us, to let them know that they are not alone.

This book is purposefully written anonymously and for the sake of openness and transparency I want to make it perfectly clear that I am the sole author of this narrative and am simply attempting to tell my own story. Having made my living as an educator, I have chosen this format of workbook/guide to tell my story because this is the genre in which I am most familiar.

In order to stay true to my understanding and commitment to practicing the 12 steps in my daily affairs, I am compelled to try and stay as anonymous as I can in order to conform in both practice and spirit to the very best intentions of the principles of anonymity as described in the book Alcoholics Anonymous. However, I will readily make my identity known for purposes of authentication and verification of source or for any other valid reason but, never, ever for self-promotion.

I have intentionally chosen to use the collective "we" rather than the singular "I" when describing what I did and what happened as the result. I do this because I did not travel the recovery path alone. In fact, I tried to apply myself to the 12 steps precisely the way my sponsors who guided me had done themselves, in their own time, and as did their sponsors before them. I simply tried to use the accounts of their own experiences as my personal recovery map and follow their actions in this now well-travelled path to freedom better known intimately and personally today by several million people living in over 190 countries around the world and in at least 40 different languages and dialects.

To anyone in need please consider this guide as potentially a map for you; to help guide your own steps forward.

Without knowing in advance, this map has led me to exactly the place I need to be today. The fact is, today I enjoy membership in a continually growing branch of God's universal family called Alcoholics Anonymous. And even more importantly, this is just one of many homes to me today that are all filled with light, love, and goodness. Being happy, joyous and free is the rule for living each and every day. I have no doubt that it can do the same for you.

So to you the reader, being a friend who I have just not yet met; I extend a warm welcome to you. Please come and join us on this broad highway to a better life. If you have read this far, then I suspect that you have something more than just a casual interest in the topic. If that be the case then please be assured that you are making your start right now.

You hold in your hand a key to a doorway that offers you a new beginning and that may offer you a pathway of hope and healing towards a life you may have never dreamed was even faintly possible. Please join us now on the broad highway to recovery.

WEEKLY MEETING AGENDA

The following is suggestive only. This is a 14 week format that works well for us when working the steps in a group setting. All readings come from the first 164 pages of the "Big Book" of Alcoholics Anonymous, except for step 7 which comes from the AA book titled "The Twelve Steps and Twelve Traditions". Our preference is to listen together to the weekly readings from the audio Big Book rather than reading individually. We have found that a 90 minute meeting with a ten minute break at mid-point works well and will allow for about 10 participants to share meaningfully at each meeting.

Meeting # & Topic	Readings
1. Commitment Meeting	Preface and all Forewords
2. Step 1	The Doctor's Opinion
3. Step 1	Ch.2 There is a Solution
4. Step 1	Ch.3 More About Alcoholism
5. Step 2	Ch.4 We Agnostics
6. Step 3	Ch.5 How it Works p.58-63
7. Step 4	Ch.5 How it Works p.63-71
8. Step 5	Ch.6 Into Action p.72-75
9. Steps 6&7	12 Steps and 12 Traditions
10. Steps 8&9	Ch.6 Into Action p.76-84
11. Steps 10&11	Ch.6 Into Action p.84-88
12. Step 12	Ch.7 Working With Others
13. Step 12	Ch.9 The Family Afterward
14. Step 12 & Farewell	Ch.11 A Vision for You

COMMITMENT MEETING

*I am not what I should be
And not what I want to be
And not what I am going to be.
But thank God!
I no longer have to stay as I am.*
~ Anonymous ~

As untreated alcoholics, the truth is that for far too long we have been the willing victim of our own disease driven lies, denials, procrastinations and wishful thinking. Any hope of recovery demands that we must start getting honest with ourselves. We will undoubtedly need help with that. That is what this guide and a good sponsor are all about.

Putting aside the oppressive and totally disabling hopelessness we were once victim to, we are now being offered a demonstrated true and very real opportunity to look into a way out of the hell hole of misery called active alcoholism. For far too long our untreated alcoholism, like any parasite, has been attacking and destroying virtually anything left in us that is good and wholesome and as the result, leaving us in a state of seemingly perpetual despair and desolation.

It has been our experience throughout our recovery that whenever we start into a new journey of uncovering, discovering, discarding and eventually recovering through the 12 step experience, we must always begin by making a personal commitment. Therefore, let us take this time to honestly ask ourselves some important questions

COMMITMENT WORKSHEET

These questions, as well as others to follow during this step series, have no right or wrong answers. They are intended to be a snapshot of where your thinking is right now. Answers of No or not sure would not be unexpected for any question. It is suggested that you answer these questions as honestly as you can and then put them away for a period of time after you have completed this step series. Then revisit them. You may be surprised with what you discover. Be diligent. Recovery is an "inside job".

1. To really give myself a chance, am I prepared to do my best to stay away from the next drink one day (or one hour if necessary) at a time, at least for the duration of this series of step taking meetings? *one incorrect?*
　　　　　　Yes ☐　　No ☐　　Not Sure ☐

2. Despite the fact that some form of crisis or possibly pressure from others may have been responsible for getting me to AA in the first place, do I now have a personal desire to try and find a real solution to my problems <u>for my sake and no one else</u>? *or thing?*
　　　　　　Yes ☐　　No ☐　　Not Sure ☐

3. Can I disregard for now any possible concern that my problems may be too different and/or too complex to be helped by AA?
　　　　　　Yes ☐　　No ☐　　Not Sure ☐

4. Can I consider with an open mind ideas and proposals that may be new and different to me?
　　　　　　Yes ☐　　No ☐　　Not Sure ☐

5. Is it possible for me to accept the idea that attending all these step meetings is of maximum importance for my recovery?

        Yes ☐   No ☐   Not Sure ☐

6. At this point, can I agree with the suggestion that some of my current thinking might well be tainted with self-denial and prejudice towards new and different ways of thinking and acting?

        Yes ☐   No ☐   Not Sure ☐

7. Can I allow myself to be open to the suggestion that my current view of myself may not be the whole truth?

        Yes ☐   No ☐   Not Sure ☐

8. Can I allow myself to be open to the suggestion that my current view of life itself may not be the whole truth?

        Yes ☐   No ☐   Not Sure ☐

9. If I do not already have one, am I willing to reach out to a trusted and experienced AA member and ask them to be my sponsor?

        Yes ☐   No ☐   Not Sure ☐

10. Am I prepared to do this more than once if necessary?

        Yes ☐   No ☐   Not Sure ☐

11. If my sponsor is available, am I prepared to meet with him/her on an ongoing basis to have questions answered and experiences shared between the step meetings?

        Yes ☐   No ☐   Not Sure ☐

12. Am I willing to make the following commitment personally and privately to myself (you may wish to share this with your sponsor) with the hope of finding an answer to my current difficulties? "I make the commitment to myself to attend every meeting of this step

series and make the promise to myself to do the very best I can at carrying out all the suggestions presented to me in the Big Book even if I may have some honest doubts?"
                  Yes ☐   No ☐   Not Sure ☐

Having now made a commitment to ourselves to give these 12 steps an honest effort from start to finish, we are ready to direct our attention specifically to step one, including the worksheet questions there to determine where we are in our thinking right now. That knowledge will clearly direct us to what we will have to do next.

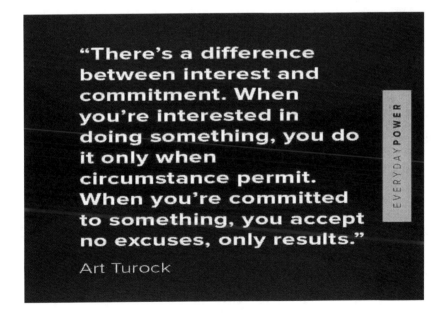

A SPECIAL MESSAGE FOR THE NEWCOMER

So, here we are; likely at a time and place we had absolutely no interest in being at when we were younger and still hopeful. No doubt this state of affairs was never on our "bucket list." There can be little doubt that along with experiencing some personal shame, there is also considerable humiliation and embarrassment. If that be the case then please know that this is perfectly normal and there is little doubt that you are exactly where you need to be at this moment.

Let us reassure you that by getting to this point, you undoubtedly have overcome the single biggest barrier you likely will ever have to face going forward. That barrier you crossed was the barrier of denial that when present makes us unreachable as far as accessing help.

By reaching out, you have performed an act of true humility. Humility is a good thing and very different from the humiliation you are no doubt too familiar with. You will learn much, much more about humility as you progress in your recovery.

For now, please be assured that you are on your way to a much more satisfying and comfortable way of life. Despite your anxiety, all you need to continue is to nurture and maintain the willingness to proceed. Let's get started on the road to sobriety and wellness.

Let the Journey Begin!

PART I: FINDING REAL RECOVERY
(Steps One to Nine)

STEP ONE

We admitted we were powerless over alcohol-that our lives had become unmanageable.

It must never be forgotten that the purpose of Alcoholics Anonymous is to sober up alcoholics. There is no religious or spiritual requirement for membership. No demands are made on anyone. An experience is offered which members may accept or reject. That is up to them.

~ Bill W ~

In our fellowship, the twelve traditions tell us that the personality (individual) is never to be featured ahead of our principles. However, some individuals attract significant positive attention because of the way they lived their life. Mychal Judge was in fact one of those very special people. Demonstrations of "good, sober living" are of priceless value to those of us trying to find our own recovery. Actions speak louder than words. As Emerson tells us; "*what you are shouts so loudly I cannot hear a word you say.*"

Father Mychal Judge was chaplain of the NYFD and a member of Alcoholics Anonymous. He lost his life on 9/11/2001 while selflessly tending to the needs of others.

Father Mychal's personal prayer is well known to the firefighters of New York City as well as the local AA community.

MYCHAL'S PRAYER

Lord; take me where you want me to be;
Help me find those you want me to meet;
Tell me what you want me to say;
And keep me out of your way.

Having now made a commitment to ourselves to give these 12 steps an honest effort from start to finish and leaving concerns about our progress or possible results aside for the time being, we are now ready to direct our attention specifically to the step one worksheet questions. Doing so will make it possible for us to determine where we are right now in our thinking. This knowledge will then direct us to what we will need to do next.

The first step asks us to accept something that appears to be a paradox: Yes: It is true: We must first admit defeat in order to claim victory later. We have now arrived at the point "where the rubber meets the road." We are squarely faced with addressing step one. We have talked "the talk"; now it is time to walk "the walk". At this point, if we are alcoholic and wish to do something about it, we must be willing to seriously consider the possibility that we are now truly powerless as far as alcohol is concerned.

We are now ready to ask ourselves some very personal and essential questions about step one which states, *"We admitted we were powerless over alcohol - that our lives had become unmanageable"*. We want to find out precisely what step one really does, or does not, mean to us at this moment in time. If we are honest with ourselves, our answers to these questions will undoubtedly provide us with insight and direction concerning what we do next.

Before we can set a new course for change we must first find out exactly where we are. Only then can we even hope to chart a new course and start moving in the right direction.

When you get into a tight place and everything goes against you, till it seems you could not hang on a minute longer, never give up then, for that is just the place and time that the tide will turn."

~ Harriet Beecher Stowe ~

STEP 1: WORKSHEET

1. Am I convinced that I have lost the power to choose whether I will drink or not? I cannot stop from drinking on my own?
Yes ☑ No ☐ Not Sure ☐

2. Am I convinced that I have an illness or disease? I am sick mentally (the obsession that I will someday be able to control my drinking and that my drinking behavior is normal), physically (I am allergic to alcohol: A craving for more develops with each drink) and spiritually (excessive thought of self; egocentric; self will run riot).
Yes ☑ No ☐ Not Sure ☐

3. Am I convinced that my illness is progressive? If I continue to drink, over any considerable period of time it always gets worse, never better.
Yes ☑ No ☐ Not Sure ☐

4. Am I convinced that my illness left untreated, can only end in insanity or premature death. Like untreated cancer, it is a consumer of mind and body.
Yes ☑ No ☐ Not Sure ☐

5. Am I convinced my illness is incurable, but it can be arrested by staying away from the first drink? "Once an alcoholic- Always an alcoholic".
Yes ☑ No ☐ Not Sure ☐

6. Am I convinced that I must stop taking that "first drink"? One is too many and twenty is not enough.
Yes ☑ No ☐ Not Sure ☐

7. Am I convinced that I cannot stop drinking on the basis of self-knowledge alone? My own will power cannot keep me sober on a long term continuing basis.
    Yes ☐ No ☐ Not Sure ☑

8. Am I convinced that I can never drink alcohol safely again. Each and every day I must have the thought and feeling that I do not want to drink today.
    Yes ☑ No ☐ Not Sure ☐

9. Am I convinced that I want to stop? I only have to stop drinking one day at a time, just for today.
    Yes ☑ No ☐ Not Sure ☐

10. Am I convinced that if I should gain a significant amount of sobriety (one week or more), and I pick up that first drink again, I would in a short time, be in the same or worse condition that I was when I quit drinking the last time.
    Yes ☑ No ☐ Not Sure ☐

11. Am I convinced that I can only be defeated by an attitude of intolerance or belligerent denial (closed mind).
    Yes ☐ No ☐ Not Sure ☑

12. Am I convinced that honesty, open mindedness and willingness (the H.O.W. of AA) are the essential tools of recovery and are indispensable.
    Yes ☑ No ☐ Not Sure ☐

13. As Herbert Spencer said, I am convinced that I would remain in everlasting ignorance if I was to have <u>contempt</u> for the complete program of recovery before I investigated it fully.
    Yes ☑ No ☐ Not Sure ☐

14. Am I convinced that no matter how complex or pressing my living problems may be; they can only be addressed effectively after the alcohol problem is dealt with.

Yes ☑ No ☒ Not Sure ☒

15. Am I convinced of the reality of my condition, not the way I think it is or would like it to be? That reality is; that I am powerless over alcohol and cannot guarantee my behavior after the first drink. The medical word for a person who has this condition of mind and body is alcoholic.

Yes ☑ No ☐ Not Sure ☐

At this point, if you have answered these questions honestly, you should now have a better idea of what you will want to do next. Please notice I just used the phrase *"want to"*. If, in fact, you can recognize within yourself this sense of *wanting* to proceed instead of just needing to, then be assured that you are truly now on your way into recovery.

If this is not the case then another closer look at step one, with your sponsor's help if possible, is probably in order along with a frank and possibly a more honest conversation with him or her would be highly recommended.

To open our minds to new ideas and/or possibilities, as uncomfortable as it may seem, is the key to the doorway leading us to recovery and wellness. Without this key, we are forever trapped in that all too familiar helpless and hopeless state of mind, body and spirit.

~Anonymous~

> **When we admit our powerlessness and our inability to manage our own lives, we open the door to recovery.**
>
> ~Basic Text, Page 19

The reason why many of us are still troubled, still seeking, still making little forward progress is because we haven't yet come to the end of <u>ourselves</u>. We're still trying to give orders, and interfering with God's work within us."

~A.W. Tozer~

Let's take a little time to pause and reflect on the following beautiful gift provided to us by our First Nations brothers and sisters.

A NATIVE AMERICAN PRAYER

*Great Spirit: Whose voice I hear in the winds.
Whose breath gives life to the entire world: Please hear me.
I am small and I am weak.
I need your strength and wisdom.*

*Let me walk in your beauty.
Let my eyes ever behold the red and purple
sunset that you have created for me.*

*Make my hands respect the things you have made.
Make my ears sharp to hear your words.
Let me learn the lessons for me that you have hidden
under every leaf and rock.*

*I seek your strength not to be greater than my brother
but rather to fight my greatest enemy – myself.*

*Make me always ready to come to you with clean hands
and straight eyes so that when my life fades as the
setting sun, my spirit can come home to you without
shame.*

~source unknown~

STEP TWO

Came to believe that a power greater than ourselves could restore us to sanity.

"Nothing can be more demoralizing than a clinging and abject dependence upon another human being. This often amounts to the demand for a degree of protection and love that no one could possibly satisfy. So our hoped for protectors finally flee, and once more we are left alone - either to grow up or to disintegrate."

~ Bill W. ~

"Your vision will become clear only when you can look into your own heart. Who looks outside, dreams; who looks inside, awakes."

~ Carl Jung ~

By now we have spent some considerable time focusing on the first step. If it is the case that we are now open to at least the first part of step one at a personal level, and that powerlessness over alcohol is definitely a part of our reality, then we will find ourselves motivated to move forward to investigate step two. (The second part of step one will be dealt with in detail later.)

Because both physical and psychological safety and security is an instinctive and universal basic need, one piece of the baggage that is a part of the suffering experienced by all human beings is the fact that new experiences can often pose a threat to our personal sense of security and of course our wellbeing. This is without question because of our innate fear of the unknown. Therefore, as newcomers to AA we ask you to keep in mind that at this moment you are now in a safe place. No harm can come to you here. We ask you to open your mind to what may be some new ideas. Also, because we are doing the right thing, we need not be fearful.

We will now be asked, for the first time in this journey into recovery, to consider some possible ideas, suggestions and alternative views that may not only be new to us but very well may awaken some personal bias or prejudice.

At this point we will be challenged to open our minds and our thinking towards at least the possibility of investigating and hopefully accepting at least some of these new ideas, if not right now, then maybe later. We must do this; if for no other reason than our current set of beliefs and practices are not working.

Also, what we are being asked to consider here has a proven track record of success spanning a great many years resulting in continuous sobriety for at least 6 million people. (Conservative estimates are 3 million living + 3 million more that recovered and later passed away sober). These sober alcoholics that came before us represent all peoples, countries and religions as well as many atheists and agnostics.

Examples of twelve step recoveries are to be found today spanning literally all of humankind and extend to the four corners of our earth. Evidently not only is this disease of ours universal, the twelve step solution is equally so.

Evident as well is the fact that those that preceded us have found something we do not yet have: But, it will be available to us now if we really want it and are prepared to work for it. The 12 step plan is totally comprehensive and inclusive, never, ever exclusive or forbidden to anyone honestly seeking help. The key to success is the simple **HOW** of the 12 steps.

***H**onesty*
***O**pen Mindedness*
***W**illingness*

"What is addiction, really? It is a sign, a signal and a symptom of distress. It is a language that tells us about a plight that must be understood."

~ Alice Miller ~

STEP2: WORKSHEET

1. Am I convinced that I have to find a power greater than human power to replace the power of alcohol over my life? Yes ☑ No ☐ Not Sure ☐

2. My own code of morals or philosophy of living, however commendable it may be, is insufficient; I cannot stay comfortably sober on a continuing basis on my own.
Yes ☑ No ☐ Not Sure ☐

3. My human intelligence alone is not enough to keep me comfortably sober on a continuing basis.
Yes ☑ No ☐ Not Sure ☐

4. The idea that self-sufficiency would solve my problems did not work. Self-sufficiency means staying comfortably sober without help.

Yes ☑ No ☐ Not Sure ☐ **5.** Up until now, I have never given the spiritual life a fair hearing; spiritual meaning a belief in some power other than human power, my own power or alcohol power.
Yes ☑ No ☐ Not Sure ☐

6. Lack of power was my dilemma. My own will power, so far as alcohol is concerned, is of no use. I cannot stop drinking, or stay stopped, on will power alone.
Yes ☑ No ☐ Not Sure ☐

7. Am I convinced that believing in a "power greater than ourselves" is a strength; not a weakness.
Yes ☑ No ☐ Not Sure ☐

8. I believe that constantly believing in "a power greater than myself" will give me purpose and direction in life without alcohol. Constant means each and every day and sometimes many times during the day.
                 Yes ☑   No ☐   Not Sure ☐

9. Am I convinced that most of my ideas for living did not work; the God of reason idea does work. The God of reason idea means living a life where in I can differentiate right from wrong thus promoting right action.
                 Yes ☑   No ☐   Not Sure ☐

10. It is true that faith has been a part of my life all the way along; for example, I have faith in science when I am told that oxygen is one of the main components of air and I need it to live. This is true even though I cannot see, smell, or touch it. Yes ☑   No ☐   Not Sure ☐

11. In the final analysis only I can tap into that Higher Power that is available to all of us. I believe that deep down within me is the fundamental idea of God. I have to find the <u>Great Reality</u> deep down within myself.
                 Yes ☑   No ☐   Not Sure ☐

13. When the obsession to take the first drink has been removed, then I will have been restored to sanity (right thinking), because I will now accept the truth that it is the thoughts or ideas that occur before the first drink, not other people or circumstances, that is the insanity of my thinking.
                 Yes ☑   No ☐   Not Sure ☐

14. I am now convinced that no human power could have relieved my alcoholism.
                 Yes ☑   No ☐   Not Sure ☐

15. I am now convinced that ~~God~~ *(mn nature)* could and would do for me what I cannot do for myself if I ask ~~Him~~. I have to try it.
Yes ☑   No ☐   Not Sure ☐

16. When many thousands of AAs around the world today say that the consciousness of the presence of this Power greater than themselves is today the most important fact of their lives. This I choose to believe.
Yes ☑   No ☐   Not Sure ☐

17. Because of my deeply rooted negative mental habits, I am convinced that I will have to ask for help every day and sometimes several times during the day if I am to recreate my life.
Yes ☑   No ☐   Not Sure ☐

"Life can be lived by denying faith or life can be lived by embracing faith. I have tried both and the latter is far more comfortable".

~Anonymous~

Gathering information by reading about a new suggestion and talking about it with others is a vital and essential precursor to actually putting it into action. Learning about a 12 step action is one thing. However, doing a step requires making a permanent change in one's conscious behavior. Just talking about something is not actually doing it. For many of us the transition from theory to practice is a very real and challenging barrier limiting our progress not only with step two, but is equally restricting with respect to our progress with the other eleven steps.

In our experience, the only way we found it possible to actually make progress with putting action into our step taking and buying into the suggestions offered, is to make sure that for each suggestion offered we must apply the following structured process.

For each suggestion (proposal) offered, we have to honestly ask ourselves if the recommended action or line of believing is consistent with, or if you prefer, agreeable with, our currently held understanding or beliefs, or, is it in some way at odds with it. If that is the case, can we allow ourselves to be open minded and consider trying to try changing our thinking, even if just temporarily. This is the challenge. This is what recovery is all about. We need to know the truth. It is really not life (the people, events, circumstances or situations around us) that is the source of our problems. Rather, it is our interpretations (judgements) of life around us that directly influences our personal state of mind and being always. Only by knowing this can we ever find recovery and cease being helpless victims to the ebb and flow of life around us and ultimately find real peace of mind and wellbeing. We cannot change life but with help we can change our relationship with life. This is precisely what the twelve steps are designed to do.

"We may think there is willpower involved, but more likely ... change is due to wanting power. Wanting the new addiction more than the old one. Wanting the new me in preference to the person I am now."

~ George Sheehan~

What follows is the account by one of our number, of a personal step two life altering moment, resulting in a priceless outcome.

THE MIRROR
(Coming to grips with Step Two)

When I arrived at the doors of Alcoholics Anonymous I was in a pitiful state and I knew it. I was a sad, lonely, hollow shell of a human being often plagued by powerful feelings of failure, self-loathing and fear. I was very confused and even unsure as to whether or not I was even in the right place.

Thanks to the encouraging and supportive ministrations of my new found AA friends, after a relatively short period of time, I was able to identify enough with these folks that I took up my new sponsor's offer and began to work the 12 steps with him and the rest of the group at the Sunday morning step taking meetings. I was still filled with doubt and apprehension. My problems certainly continued to be overwhelming and the steps looked both perplexing and daunting. Fortunately, being without any other options, I stayed with it.

After making some modest headway with *step one*, I hit the proverbial wall with a thud. *Step two* seemed to be a complete impossibility. My view of myself and any possible connection to a Higher Power can be best summarized into two short statements.

<u>First</u>: *If there is a God; it appears to me that "He" or " She" or "It" has had little positive impact in this hate filled and ugly world as far as I could see and*

<u>Second</u>: *If there is a God why on earth would He want to have anything to do with the likes of me? In truth, I could not stand myself; why on earth would anyone else?*

Despite my reticence, but as previously noted, being out of options, in due course I did take my sponsor's advice to carefully consider the two choices offered to me on page 53 of the Big Book found in the following powerful and ultimately life altering, forty six word paragraph.

"When we became alcoholics, crushed by a self-imposed crisis, we could no longer postpone or evade. We had to fearlessly face the proposition that God is either everything, or else He is nothing, either God is or He isn't. What was our choice to be?"

It was recommended to me that if not literally, at least figuratively, I should look myself in the eye through a mirror and **honestly** find out what these two choices actually do mean to me.

Thankfully, I did take the advice. After some considerable time passed which included several false starts and some honest soul searching, I eventually came to the following understanding about step two that made real sense to me and allowed me to start to consider the rest of the plan of recovery with some real new found hope.

This is how I came to see the only two options available to me in regards to this fundamental and essential question of origins:

1. *If there is no God; then it appears to me that we might well be no more than the irrelevant and useless product of a random event that took place somewhere in an unfriendly and chaotic universe. This universe itself was evidently created by accident, out of nothing, and is apparently spinning aimlessly and without purpose towards nowhere in particular.*

Or:

2. *If God does exist; then, maybe: Just maybe: We are the product of a loving and caring Creator. This "Higher Power" that created us to be unique and purposeful, designed to live a meaningful and productive life. Our destiny is to be an integral and essential part of a universal human family wherein happiness and well-being is the norm. As well, and maybe most importantly, we are to have available to us the comfort of the conscious knowledge of His Presence, along with His infinite guidance, love and care not only for the rest of this life but for all of eternity as well. All that is asked of us is to use our free will and honestly ask for help and then most challenging of all, practice the trust that, in fact, we are getting it.*

For me, resolution did not come easily, but ultimately, my choice became obvious. I made my decision and immediately took action by specifically asking for "His" help. Then, in time, liking the results, I came to buy 110%.

Since then, I have made sure that this question is forever *"finished business"* never to be challenged again. Save for some short periods of distraction and forgetfulness resulting from my own spiritual laziness, absolutely nothing in the years since has even mildly tempted me to renege on my decision.

In hindsight I can readily see that this decision was my first conscious step towards creating a real, living, breathing, vital, personal relationship with a "Higher Power" personal to me. Today I am convinced that this decision and the commitment to take the actions that follow in step three truly opened the door to a real growing, living faith for me. I have grown comfortable enough with this Power today to simply call Him *"Father"*. (When I honestly reach out in prayer to Him today I feel like I am truly *"returning home"* where I believe I am meant to be.)

I am also convinced that this personal relationship with my Heavenly Father is what I had unknowingly and fruitlessly been searching for through the bottom of the bottle during my drinking days. This was the missing item in my makeup that had caused me to feel so uncomfortable, so incomplete, so fearful and so inadequate. If you are a seeker, like me, desperately craving to find that ever elusive "something missing" are you ready to make a choice right now? If so: *What is your choice to be?*

Belief in a Higher Power begins or is further postponed at this point; depending on how you decide to use your free will in terms of your choice of thought and intention.

Short of the occurrence of a sudden impact filled and dramatic spiritual experience, like those documented in the Big Book and which evidently have and will continue to occur to a fortunate few; for the vast majority of us, faith develops slowly over time by applying disciplined, repetitive, conscious thought. This is done through practicing purposeful meditation and prayer. This is done at predetermined times in our day and maybe more importantly at moments of spontaneity during the day when circumstances warrant. With practice the new thought (or choice of thinking) will eventually become embedded as our "default" idea or belief. This entrenched tenet then becomes a valuable "reset" button through the course of our day. Ongoing effort on our part is required. A price has to be paid for recovery. Persistent due diligence is part of that price. It is now up to you.

> *I am not what I should be and*
> *Not what I want to be and*
> *Not what I will be. But thank God:*
> *I am not what I used to be".*
>
> ~ John Newton~

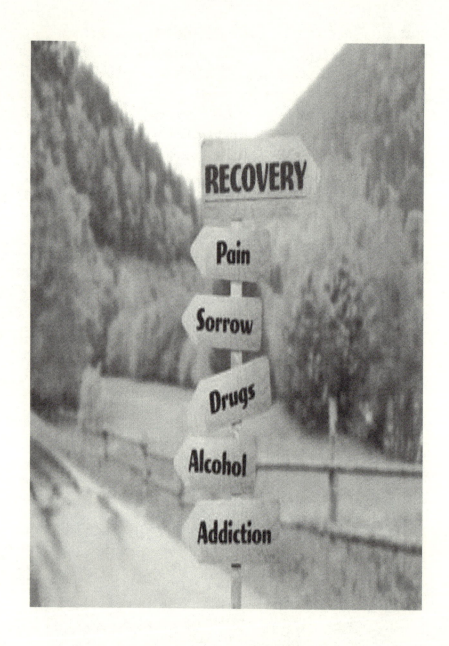

STEP THREE

Made a decision to turn our will and our life over to the care of God (as we understand Him)

"Learning how to live in the greatest peace, partnership, and brotherhood with all men and women, of whatever description, is a moving and fascinating adventure".

~ Bill W. ~

A SPECIAL MESSAGE FOR THOSE OF YOU WORKING THE STEPS FOR THE FIRST TIME

By necessity, some of the following questions making up the step 3 worksheet that follows may well go beyond your current state of mind and/or acceptance. Please do not concern yourself with any No, or Not Sure responses to any of these questions (possible exceptions may be #5, 8, 9 and 10). In any event, consult your sponsor and keep moving forward.

STEP 3: WORKSHEET

1. Am I convinced that the maintenance of a constant belief in a "Power greater than myself will give me the strength and inspiration I need to go on with the rest of the steps of recovery.

      Yes ☐   No ☐   Not Sure ☐

2. Half-measures, or taking this program in a half-hearted, or on again off again basis will avail me nothing. This I believe.

      Yes ☐   No ☐   Not Sure ☐

3. Harmful old ideas of mine that will come to my attention later in this step series, will have to be let go of absolutely otherwise progress in my recovery will be nil. This I believe.

      Yes ☐   No ☐   Not Sure ☐

4. I must go on with steps three to nine if I am to recover. Steps ten, eleven and twelve will give me the tools to live each day comfortably without the need to consume alcohol. This I believe.

Yes ☐   No ☐   Not Sure ☐

5. Life run on my own self will has not been a success; doing things my way has usually ended up with me hurting someone. This I believe.

Yes ☐   No ☐   Not Sure ☐

6. I have to develop a manner of living which demands "rigorous honesty" with myself and to apply "caring honesty" with others. Caring honesty means to apply the dictum "if you do not have something positive to say then strongly consider the option off not of not saying anything at all". This I believe.

Yes ☐   No ☐   Not Sure ☐

7. My self-centredness which often appears in such forms as self-delusion, self-seeking, self-pity and fear is the root of my troubles; my fears inevitably can be reduced to one of two concerns; either fear of losing something I already have, or fear of not getting something I feel I need or want. This I believe.

Yes ☐   No ☐   Not Sure ☐

8. My troubles are basically of my own making. I step on the toes of my fellows and they retaliate. This I believe.

Yes ☐   No ☐   Not Sure ☐

9. In some relationships, at some time in the past, I have made decisions based on self which later put me into a position to be hurt. This I believe.

          Yes ☐   No ☐   Not Sure ☐

10. I have to quit playing God because it doesn't work; playing God is trying to run the show at home, at work or at play. This I believe.

          Yes ☐   No ☐   Not Sure ☐

11. I constantly have to watch that I do not drift into worry, remorse or morbid reflection of the past. This I believe

          Yes ☐   No ☐   Not Sure ☐

12. Every night I need to constructively review my day – was I resentful, selfish, dishonest or afraid? What are the details? Do I owe an amend to someone? This I believe.

          Yes ☐   No ☐   Not Sure ☐

13. Upon awakening I have to consider my plans for the day asking that I be divorced from self-pity, dishonest or self-seeking motives. This I believe.

          Yes ☐   No ☐   Not Sure ☐

14. I made an offer of myself in the step 3 prayer and the sincerity of my decision will dictate whether or not I feel comfortable in my recovery. This I believe.

          Yes ☐   No ☐   Not Sure ☐

15. I am now convinced that self, manifesting itself in various ways, is what had defeated me; I now must consider its common manifestations and start work on step four. This I believe.

Yes ☐   No ☐   Not Sure ☐

16. The following prayer that I am going to say out loud alone or with an understanding person – is said with all the honesty I can muster at this time; "God, I offer myself to thee. To build with me and do with me as Thou wilt. Relieve me of the bondage of self, that I may better do thy will. Take away my difficulties, that victory offers them may bear witness to those I would help with Thy power, Thy love and Thy way of life. May I do Thy will always"? Amen.

Faith is taking the first step even when you don't see the whole staircase.

~ MLK ~

What follows is borrowed from Al Anon. Both of us, being victims of the same disease, allows us to share a common solution using the same simple spiritual tools.

Just for Today

JUST FOR TODAY I will try to live through this day only, and not tackle my whole life problem all at once. I can do something for twelve hours that would appall me if I felt that I had to keep it up for a lifetime.

* * *

JUST FOR TODAY I will be happy. This assumes to be true what Abraham Lincoln said, that "Most folks are as happy as they make up their minds to be."

* * *

JUST FOR TODAY I will adjust myself to what is, and not try to adjust everything else to my own desires. I will take my "luck" as it comes, and fit myself to it.

* * *

JUST FOR TODAY I will try to strengthen my mind. I will study. I will learn something useful. I will not be a mental loafer. I will read something that requires effort, thought and concentration.

STEP THREE: **WHY NOT GIVE IT A TRY?**

The short form of step three says *"Made a decision to turn our will and lives over to the care of God as we understood Him"*. The starting point here obviously is to make that decision, as suggested. Making this decision is a vital and essential starting point in our effort to come to grips with step three. However, in making this decision, it is paramount that we realize that absolutely nothing of a personally transforming nature will ever happen in regards to step three until we actually put that decision into action.

We who make this statement have continually found, in our own spiritual journey, that God (as we understand Him) is the perfect gentleman. He does not intrude anywhere He is not invited. This means, that we have to make a conscious request for help to Him, followed by a conscious surrender of personal control over the specific event or situation of concern. Truly, half-measures will avail us nothing in this regard.

For we who are of agnostic disposition, it can seem beyond the realm of possibility, to suddenly and completely abandon the reins of personal control to a higher authority. Especially one that is still very new and mostly unknown to us. The fact is, this Higher Power idea is still something totally unproven and without corroboration in our personal experience to date.
Our belief in a Higher Power at this point is based on little more than some new found hope provided to us in the form of anecdotal evidence and affirmations heard from others at AA meetings who are sharing their own experience. In the legal sense, our evidence to date is strictly circumstantial and based entirely on speculation and hearsay.

Circumstantial evidence would be very difficult for a courtroom jury to base a conclusion on let alone an anxious, newly sober alcoholic, who, at the moment, may not be too tightly wrapped. Our current situation, regardless of just how ineffective and troublesome it is, is at least familiar. We often opt for the familiarity of the status quo rather than face the fear always associated with the unknown.

Most of us have faced this conundrum and consequently exercised some considerable foot dragging because we truly did not know how to overcome this formidable challenge. That being said, let's take a moment to hear from one of our own, who, following a suggestion from another, was ultimately able to begin to transform his step three decision from theory into very real and effective action.

"To actually put step three into practice required me to literally make a leap of faith. This was most definitely something I was not used to doing and which caused me some considerable angst, uncertainty and fear. I have to admit that I stewed in my own juices about this for quite some time. It seems that my problem specifically was that I was unable to differentiate between trying to climb the whole mountain of that thing called faith in one gigantic leap rather than to figure out how to make the first step.

Thankfully, in AA, help is not far away, if we are looking for it. As memory serves me, I found myself talking with friends in the parking lot after a regular weekly meeting. Because it was a common practice of mine in those days, in all likelihood I was grousing about my continuing inability to actually put step three into practice. My dilemma was that even though I was able to concede that intellectually I agreed in principle with the step, I was unable to put it into practice. I still had no trust in uncertainty.

One of the elder statesmen in the group spoke up at that point. I suspect his patience with me was being tested. As I recollect, he took a deep breath and proceeded quietly but firmly, to suggest to me that I might want to find a small, relatively benign circumstance or situation of concern in my life that is not in the "life or death" category of problems and to then try consciously to surrender that circumstance and eventual outcome specifically into God's hands and then just wait and see what happens? In other words, try this faith thing out in a safe way!
I am sure that it was not more than a day or two later, while starting the day's activities at work, I did find myself preoccupied with worry about some particular (but now long forgotten) issue on the radar for that morning. At that point what had been suggested to me in the AA parking lot suddenly came to mind. And because time was short, and without any further thought, I consciously and quickly

consciously surrendered this specific worry into God's hands. Then the day started to happen and my attention was by necessity re-focused outward and I thought no more of the matter.

Later that day, while I was enjoying a welcome moment of calm and reflection, my early morning surrender came to mind. It was at that moment that I also recognized the fact that the morning had passed delightfully smoothly. The expected troubles had not come to pass as anticipated.

I believe that a common reaction of mine at this point would normally have been to simply write the whole thing off to good luck. Fortunately for me, this time, I did not do that. Instead, I instantly thought of the promise to all of us found in pertinent idea (c) on page 60 of our Big Book that says "God could and would (help) if He was sought."

At that moment I somehow knew that this erstwhile insignificant experience was really important for me to remember. My guess is that I hoped that this was possibly one of those special, memorable events sometimes called "AHA" moments that others had often talked about at meetings. The passage of time has proven this to be true.

Today, I understand that moment to be a clear example of the result of a positive change in thinking. More importantly, I identify that event as a confirming example of direct personal evidence of a God personal to me answering a specific prayer for help. It truly was a moment of awakening.

I have never forgotten that first tentative conscious effort of trying to practice faith and it has become the foundation stone upon which an ever growing number of personal examples of God's love, grace and guidance have come to my attention and continue to bring more and more wellness, personal fulfillment and spiritual trust into my life.

I prefer to believe that for the first time in my life, this moment of revelation occurred specifically because I was able to open my spiritual eyes and actually see what had previously been invisible to me. I believe that I was spiritually blind until that very moment. Like a new pair of prescription glasses, a whole new world of vast beauty, magnificent colours and endless love has ever so slowly grown into focus. As the result of this experience my life was and is permanently changed.

I am most richly blessed. I know today that my personal experience is not at all unusual or rare in the fellowship of Alcoholics Anonymous. Like any journey of 1000 miles, this spiritual journey also begins with the first step. More often than not that first step must be a baby step."

Let us never forget that the practicing of each and every one of these suggested twelve steps requires a cognitive response (conscious mental effort) on our part. Recovery begins as a process of inside change. For many of us, recovery is a slow process that involves the wholesale replacement of our fundamental beliefs, perceptions and interpretations of life around us. Ultimately, recovery demands a complete change in our view of ourselves and our relationship to the world around us. It will take time.

These essential changes are beyond our ability to do alone. Only God's help can make these changes possible. That is exactly what the 12 steps of recovery are designed to facilitate for us. It always works for anyone of us who is prepared to totally buy into the AA program of recovery and put in the effort. Always remember that because yesterday is gone and tomorrow is not here yet, the only thing we really have is today.

The price of recovery demands that each of us taking the time each and every day, as well as multiple times throughout the day, to once again, consciously surrender our will and our life into God's hands.
We also ask for the insight and courage to do the next right thing in each circumstance we face.
We ask to be relieved of our selfish desires so we can better do His will.
We ask to be grateful for our life for this day and the opportunity to make a positive difference to the lives of the people we meet.
By practicing self-discipline in this manner over the course of time, we, in fact, do transform our flawed, ineffective and self-defeating ways of diseased thinking into a healthy, positive and wellness creating mind.

The really good news here is that not only does it work beautifully for those using the conventional religious model of a higher power it also works just as well for any honest personal conception of a power greater than one's self. This Power must always be totally inclusive: It can never be exclusive or forbidding.

Finally, and for the purpose of emphasis, let us never forget that the practicing of each and every one of these suggested twelve steps requires a cognitive response (conscious mental action). Recovery is a process of internal change. Recovery involves the altering of our fundamental thinking. This includes all beliefs, perceptions and interpretations of life around us. These changes are beyond our ability to do alone. Only God can make these changes in us. This is exactly what the 12 steps of recovery are designed to facilitate for us. It always works for anyone who is prepared to totally buy in to the AA program of recovery and then put in the required effort.

SOME PRICELESS AND TIMELY SUGGESTIONS

Speak as little as possible of one's self.
Mind one's own business.
Accept contradictions and correct them cheerfully.
Pass over the mistakes of others.
Accept being slighted, forgotten and disliked.
Be kind and gentle even under provocation

~Ste. Teresa of Calcutta~

"Humiliation is painful and a symptom of disease.
Humility is a precursor to peace and is a vital component of wellness.

~Anonymous~

STEPS FOUR AND FIVE

(4) Made a searching and fearless moral inventory of ourselves. (5) Admitted to God, to ourselves and another human being the exact nature of our wrongs.

"We know that permanent sobriety can be attained only by a most revolutionary change in the life and outlook of the individual."

~ Bill W. ~

Confront the dark parts of yourself and work to banish them by illuminating them and sharing them with another person and then accept the divine forgiveness inherent in doing so. Your willingness to wrestle with your demons will cause your angels to sing.

~ August Wilson ~

In order to complete a successful personal inventory, there are a number of questions to be asked before beginning as well as some clearly defined goals and expectations to be aware of. Please consider the following questions and suggestions carefully. As with all the other worksheets in this guide, your honest answers to these questions will tell you more about your current state of mind and what you need to do next in your search for recovery than anything else you might try.

Open your mind to new suggestions, trust your instincts and give it your best effort. Remember; for any endeavor, outcomes are the direct product of the effort put in.

STEP 4: WORKSHEET

1. Am I now ready to begin the process of facing and getting rid of the things in my past that have been blocking me from a Higher Power?

    Yes ☐ No ☐ Not Sure ☐

2. Can I make every effort to be open and honest with myself when reviewing my past?

    Yes ☐ No ☐ Not Sure ☐

3. Am I now convinced that self, manifested in various ways, is what has defeated me?
    Yes ☐ No ☐ Not Sure ☐

4. Am I now willing to look for and consider the common manifestations of self in my own past behavior?
    Yes ☐ No ☐ Not Sure ☐

5. Resentments being the number one offender am I now ready to set them all down on paper.
    Yes ☐ No ☐ Not Sure ☐

6. Am I prepared to go back through my life thoroughly and honestly to identify and record my self-generated "damaged goods?"
    Yes ☐ No ☐ Not Sure ☐

7. With each of the resentments identified, am I willing to ask God to help me deal with them?
    Yes ☐ No ☐ Not Sure ☐

8. With persons to whom I am resentful, can I begin to practice the same tolerance, pity and patience I would cheerfully grant a sick friend?
    Yes ☐ No ☐ Not Sure ☐

9. Can I now make every effort to avoid any further retaliation and argument towards such persons?
    Yes ☐ No ☐ Not Sure ☐

10. Am I prepared to put aside the wrongs others have done and resolutely look for my own mistakes?
        Yes ☐   No ☐   Not Sure ☐

11. When I find such faults will I list them on paper?
        Yes ☐   No ☐   Not Sure ☐

12. Am I prepared to admit these faults honestly and am I willing to try and set these matters straight?
        Yes ☐   No ☐   Not Sure ☐

13. Can I honestly review my past and record those situations in which fear raises its ugly head?
        Yes ☐   No ☐   Not Sure ☐

14. In such cases can I now conclude that my fear was primarily based on the fact that self-reliance had failed me?
        Yes ☐   No ☐   Not Sure ☐

15. Can I now begin to substitute a trust in God for self-reliance? Can I now begin to trust infinite God rather than my finite self?
        Yes ☐   No ☐   Not Sure ☐

16. Can I now accept the following statement? "Just to the extent that I do as I think He would have me, and humbly rely on Him, does He enable me to match calamity with serenity."
        Yes ☐   No ☐   Not Sure ☐

17. Am I now prepared to accept without reservation the following truth? "The verdict of the ages is that faith means courage. All women and men of faith have courage. They trust their God. They never apologize for their God. Instead they let Him demonstrate through them what He can do."

Yes ☐   No ☐   Not Sure ☐

18. I am a person of faith. Therefore I claim access to courage.

Yes ☐   No ☐   Not Sure ☐

I now ask the God of my understanding to remove my fears and direct my attention to what He would have me be, so that I might begin to outgrow my fears.

A PRAYER OF SURRENDER

Lord, I give you this mountain of fear that I feel inside. Sometimes life overwhelms me and I feel overcome by anxiety and doubt.

Lord, the storms of life have come and rocked this boat I journey in. I open my heart to receive Your grace.

Lord, fill me with boldness to step off this shaking ship and greet you on the waters of life. My feet are sinking and my heart is fearful.

Lord, I take Your hand and I give You these things that I am most afraid of. Teach me and show me how I can trust You more.

Lord, please save me!

~ Anonymous ~

To help you prepare to do a successful personal inventory, please consider the following four suggestions.

1. You will never be totally ready to take this step nor can you expect to do this task perfectly. This kind of thinking is used by some of us as an excuse to never get started or at least never get ready to move on. So get rid of any such thinking right now. Get your ego out of the way, if only for the time being.

2. *"But I don't have time in my busy life to do this properly."* Not true! With your sponsor's help, plan out a period of time in the next week or two, of absolutely no more than eight hours, hopefully much less. This time is for you to be able to devote your full attention to the step four task in the manner described below. This predetermined time can either be used all at once, or broken up into smaller pieces. Whatever works best for you. After doing so as honestly as you can, you must consider the task finished (for now). It is now time to prepare to do step five.

3. Before you begin; and with your sponsor's help if needed, arrange an appointment with the person of your choice to hear your inventory. This will give you a deadline for helping get your personal inventory done and also be a helpful motivator for you.

4. Am I really ready to do this thing? *"Yes I am anxious and even a little fearful and would prefer to not do this humbling action (perfectly normal at this point) but I know that I must if I want to get better"*. If you are not willing to agree with this statement then you must come clean and save both your sponsor and yourself from wasting valuable time. Your time will be better spent reassessing your priorities by re-visiting steps one to three.

Remember that we need to find some real fun and enjoyment in what we are doing in this journey or we will not stay with it. Being sad, morose and self-deprecating will not be tolerated any more. Let us pause for a moment and enjoy Steve's perspective on his recovery.

Today I want to live my life in such a way that when I wake up in the morning the devil says "Ah shit; he's up."

~ Steve Maraboli ~

*To get started with your step four personal inventory, prepare several sheets of paper with the column headings shown below and follow the instructions .

MY PERSONAL INVENTORY

(Be diligent! Be honest! Trust in God! You are not alone!)

RESENTMENTS	WHAT THEY DID	WHY I AM ANGRY	MY FAULTS
Includes people places or institutions that when thought of, cause feelings of anger, agitation, regret, anxiety or any other form of unease	What did they do or what is it about them that caused you discomfort? In other words, what were their faults?	Wherever possible, state why this person or situation is unsettling to you. What is it about your wellbeing that is being threatened here? Is it your security, your self-image and/or your public-image or your sense of self-worth and/or identity that is being threatened here?	Now that you have identified how you have been wronged: In each case try and identify specifically where you were at fault. Ultimately all faults distill down to three simple questions: Was I selfish? Was I dishonest? Was I afraid?

Begin with the first column. Starting with your life today and working backwards in time. List every person, place or principle that causes you any mental unrest at all when you think of them/it. Places or institutions that may be relevant would include church, marriage, banks, and police/courts. Complete the 2nd and 3rd columns as specifically and briefly as you can. Do not dwell on puzzling or questionable situations. Move on and come back later. Don't over think at this point.

Now go back over what you have done so far and in the last column, indicate your (not their) faults are in each instance. In their simplest form, faults can be identified as being in one of only three categories, Selfishness, dishonesty or fear. As previously noted, fear is of only two types. 1. Fear of losing something you already have or 2. Fear of not getting something you need or feel you deserve. Then take the time to reflect carefully on all that you have written

THE ISSUE OF FEAR

"Concerning the question of fear, only the self-deceived will claim perfect freedom from fear."

~ Bill W. ~

Thankfully; no one is immune to fear. I say thankfully because the conscious response of fear is one of the essential items making up humanity's instinctive package of survival tools. We live in a world full of unpredictability, hazards of all kinds and other dangerous circumstances. Because many of these threats have the capability of materializing suddenly with little or no warning, we need our innate and speedy reflex responses along with the hormonally generated conscious feeling of fear in order to respond quickly and appropriately to the initial threat and to then be prompted to take other appropriate conscious acts of safety.

As well, the experience of fear acts as a trigger or reminder later when circumstances are safe and secure for us to learn from the event by consciously reviewing and evaluating the fear causing circumstances to hopefully avoid similar future threats. The immediate and long term value of the fear response in its appropriate place is undeniably essential for every individual's survival.

However, the problem with the fear response that we alcoholics, and addicts have is that we suffer this symptom excessively and often at inappropriate and unnecessary times. For reasons addressed later in this essay, fear inevitably becomes a much too common and debilitating companion in our daily lives. The incapacitating response of fear, as described in the Big

Book of Alcoholics Anonymous, *"an evil and corroding thread shot through the entire fabric of our lives"* has unfortunately become an unbearable reality in all of our lives. By the way, this unhealthy level of fear is also one of the unbearable burdens common to all who are afflicted with clinical depression and anxiety regardless of the causes or circumstances. When this happens, we have become an unwitting and helpless victim to life instead of a healthy participant in life.

If we are to ever achieve anything even approaching a healthy psyche, we are going to have to get rid of this debilitating burden. Fortunately, completing our step four will help us begin to do just that.

To help us identify the fear that is in our step four, let us first identify the causes or sources of all fears. This will help us recognize more easily the incidences of fear in our lives.

The fact is, fear will immediately make its presence known whenever one or more of our basic human needs are threatened. Psychologists tell us that all humans have three basic requirements or needs that have to be fulfilled to our own satisfaction before we can experience any significant level of true well-being and peace of mind. An acronym of these three essentials for mental wellness could be simply **"The 3S's"**. In no particular order they are:

Security: Which includes all of our personal, physical, psychological and/or emotional wellbeing or the lack thereof?

Situation: How we perceive ourselves (who am I?) and how we interpret our relationship with the world in which we live (Is it positive or negative?).

Significance: Specifically meaning our sense of purpose, usefulness and value. (Is it good or bad?)

Whenever any one or more of these criteria are even perceived as being under threat, we are immediately immersed in fear and it will remain unabated until all such threat(s) are eliminated.

Please note that the operational word here is *perceived*. Whether a threat is real or not is of no real importance to the individual in question. Simply put, our conscious connection to the world outside, the so called "real world", is only possible through the information (data) received by our subconscious brain via our five sets of sensory receptors followed by the interpretation, evaluation and codification of that information by our conscious brain. Our understanding of the world in which we live is no more or less than our personal interpretation of this data as the perceived circumstances. Because we all do this a little differently; this is why there are often many different opinions or accounts of the same event or phenomenon.

Now, at this point, we ask you to go back to your step four writings and add a fifth column to the right hand side of your page(s) under the heading of FEARS. Then, add a checkmark beside each of the resentments you described that include the element of personal fear. Also, if possible, indicate if the fear was the result of a threat to your security, your significance, your situation or some combination of those three. By doing this we can help ourselves appreciate just how pervasive, intrusive and damaging fear has been in our lives. Truly that evil and corroding thread Bill referenced earlier. Steps five through twelve will guide us as to how to eliminate it for good.

FYI: Please remember that our only connection to reality, whatever reality may be, is our perception or interpretation of what is happening around us. This is because, metaphorically speaking, we all see and interpret life's events through our own set of filters. Everyone's filters are somewhat different from everyone else, even identical twins. If this was not the case then there would never be any disagreement in interpretation of reality. There is no doubt that all of us will always have a distorted or incomplete understanding of reality due to ingrained biases, misunderstandings, prejudices, and simply lack of complete knowledge. For anyone to think otherwise would be total folly.

Finally, at this point the Big Book asks us do address the question of possible sex problems in our life. If you feel that you need some further help with this, talk to your sponsor about any concerns. If you are honest with yourself, you will know what you need to do.

Finally: We have one further request of you, which possibly may turn out to be the single most healing action you will ever take in the whole process.

Please write down in your inventory, for only God, yourself and one other human being to see/hear, that ONE thought or memory in your mind that despite all your efforts you can never forget and that you find so personally humiliating and distasteful, that you have vowed, up until now, to never share with another human being.

We would hardly be human if we did not have at least one such haunting memory.

We implore you with only your best interests in mind to please, please, do this and share it with that other human being in your step five. You have carried this dreadful baggage for far too long. This is the one thing that, unless addressed in this fashion will forever keep you separated from the *"sunlight of your spirit"* and all the wellness that flows from it. Do this with the confidence that because you are doing the right thing, you do not walk alone. God already knows. You must tell another human being: For your own sake!

Of course, within the fellowship, we always share our experience, strength, hope and our time with each other for free and for fun. However, if we are going to see someone outside our fellowship to do your step five, we need always to remember that their time is worthy of our hire: *If you are in the position to do so*, and no other guidelines are available, you might want to ask your-self what one hour of your time is worth to you as a possible guide to determining appropriate compensation to that other person for helping you.

You are now ready to go forth eager, happy and unafraid to
Complete your step five and lift the unbearable burden of these stifling and oppressive emotional anchors. All of us who have preceded you are with you in spirit, thought and prayer. *God is always with you.*

When we allow our faith to become bigger than our fears then an endless world of opportunities becomes open to us and we will know true peace of mind.

~Anonymous~

SIMPLY FOR CLARITY OF AND UNDERSTANDING BETWEEN YOU AND ME

Our understanding of the words *reality* and *truth* may not be the same as yours. What follows is our take on meanings. You are not required to endorse this point of view, only to know the 'backstory' of the message offered for the purpose of better understanding for you the reader with we, the writers.

Reality is not questionable whereas truth is questionable. Reality has nothing to do with power. It is all about authenticity. Authenticity is the proof regarding the original. Hence it can be said that reality is original. It is indeed the factor of authenticity that separates reality from truth.

On the other hand, truth is all about power. As a conclusion it can be said that it takes time for reality to become truth. How long it takes lies in the hands of man.

Man needs the power to establish the truth in the reality that has been existent for long.

God exists not only for those who believe but also for those who do not. Only one's belief in God is deniable, not His existence.

The belief that God is everywhere was sown right from the moment when man appeared and there are numerous religions and beliefs that have sprung up since then. But, all of them ultimately point to the truth that there is a supreme power above all of us that controls everything.

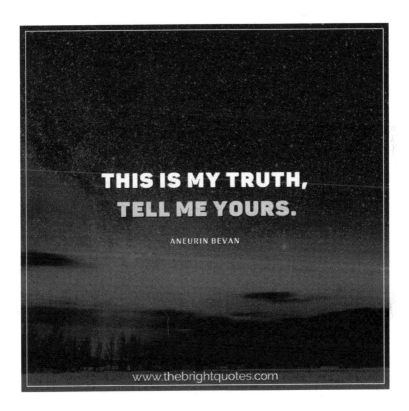

STEPS SIX AND SEVEN

(6) We're entirely ready to have God remove all these defects of character. (7) Humbly asked Him to remove our shortcomings.

"I try hard to hold fast to the truth that a full and thankful heart cannot entertain great conceits. When brimming with gratitude, one's heartbeat must surely result in outgoing love, the finest emotion we can ever know."

~Bill W~

Let's be very clear as we begin work on these steps. Studying a step and actually taking a step are two very different things. Reading about a new suggestion or idea and talking about it with others is essential as a precursor to actually taking the essential actions required. The actions demand us to somehow facilitate and implement a positive change in our conscious behavior. For many of us this transition from theory to practice is a very real and very challenging barrier limiting our progress not only with steps six and seven, but also equally restricting with respect to our progress with the other eleven steps.

In our experience, the only way we found it possible to actually make progress with the implementation of these steps relative to changing our thinking was to make sure that in each case, we had identified as clearly and as simply as possible each and every option and course of action available to us concerning the step's suggested mental actions. Then, with careful consideration of the consequences inherent in each thought option, it becomes possible to properly compare and evaluate these mental models or choices of actions. In this case, only then will the appropriate model or plan of action of doing steps six and seven become clear to us. At this point we will be finally able to start to consciously put these new thoughts into practice.

With the assurance of having done our due diligence we are motivated to continue to do so until results begin to provide us with personal evidence of success and which will instill still more confidence. In the final analysis, as far as steps six and seven are concerned, ***it is only by conscious mental practice that we can replace the negative with the positive in our thinking.***

What follows is an affirmation of this truth. Some define this statement as a poem, others as a prayer. This of course is a personal matter and makes no difference whatsoever to the truth inherent in the message. Our perceptions and thinking about our life up to this point has not been the result of our experiences, it has been the cause of those experiences. Whether we ultimately determined them to be good or bad is inconsequential. If we are to ever be able to experience the joy of living instead of pain, loneliness and inadequacy, we must look inward to make that change, not outward.

AS I THINK: I AM

*I am today where my thoughts
have brought me;
I will be tomorrow where my thoughts
take me.
I cannot escape the results
of my thoughts,
But I can endure and learn; I can accept
and I can be glad.*

*I will always realize that which
is in my heart:
Be it base or beautiful,
or a mixture of both:
I will always gravitate towards that
which I most covet.
Into my hands will be placed the exact results of
my thoughts;
I will receive that, which I earn,
no more, no less.
Whatever my present
environment may be,
I will fall, remain, or rise with
my thoughts, my vision and my attitudes.
I will become as small as
my most controlling desire,
or as great as my most lofty aspirations.
May I aspire to do better today!*

The above poem/prayer offers some real insight into why we are as we are. This concept is the foundation stone for recovery upon which the 12 steps of Alcoholics Anonymous are built. A beloved old timer (now deceased) by the name of *Chuck Chamberlain* described this truth in regards to his own recovery as being like acquiring a new pair of glasses. This is also the title of the book published after Chuck's death describing his recovery in his own words. A wonderfully insightful read if you can get your hands on a copy.

It is stated in the AA book titled *The Twelve Steps and Twelve Traditions,* that steps 6 and 7 are the steps that separate the adults from the children, or if you prefer, the truly dedicated from the pretenders. This is the point in our journey where we are challenged to ask ourselves *just how big of a price we are prepared to make to further our recovery* by buying into the spiritual way of life. Any spiritual growth demands a surrender of self-interest which, by the way, is this writer's definition of personal humility. A price has to be paid to acquire recovery.

For many of us, these two steps, six and seven, are the ones most requiring ongoing attention regardless of how far away from the last drink we may be. Unlike drinking, for which absolute hopelessness combined with total acceptance of step one made it possible for us to capitulate the drink problem completely; these other defects of character or shortcomings (same thing), seem to be impossible to completely eradicate. Being children of our ego, they continue to pop up and inevitably wreak havoc in our lives.

The AA program promises any alcoholic hoping to be less frequently burdened by this "stinking thinking" that this will happen over the course of time if one applies ongoing attention to the conscious surrendering of these shortcomings to God whenever they occur. For particularly burdensome defects, the work may seem never ending.

It is said in the other Big Book, that we will always be helped if we ask. So do not hesitate to ask:

"Seek and you shall find: Knock and the door will be opened: Ask and it shall be given".

Honest prayer never goes unanswered. On a more secular and personal level, an often stated truth in AA meetings heard around the world to this day, tells us:

"We cannot control the thoughts that pop into our head, but we are most definitely responsible for what we do with those thoughts."

We are being told here that we have to work with God in practicing steps six and seven. We cannot go it alone but God will only do for us that which we cannot do for ourselves. The facts are, triggers initiating the thoughts that pop into our head, (some external and others internal), are totally beyond any ability we think we might have to control them. So we simply have to accept such occurrences whenever they occur and whether they are good or bad. We thank Him for the positive thoughts and must ask humbly that the negative thoughts be removed.

With negative thinking, we must not passively wait for some change in our thinking to occur. We believe God wants us to do the necessary work with his help. *We will need to actively turn our attention and efforts to some sort of positive thinking and actions knowing that we will be given the necessary guidance and direction.* A positive willful act on our part is required. In that we are now not "going it alone" we can be confident of success as long as we remain diligent and continue to try to put the righteous thoughts into righteous actions.

The uncontrollability of random thoughts was first brought to our attention by a sponsor some years ago and we will be forever grateful to him because we had carried a huge amount of unnecessary guilt for a very long time.

We also know that through much of our journey in the past we have been passively carried because of our helplessness. But now, having experienced a new awakening, we can at least begin to think about what we can and must be doing to play our part in our own recovery and, along with God's guidance, try to add to the wellbeing of those around us.

"Character cannot be developed in ease and quiet. Only through experience of trial and suffering can the soul be strengthened, ambition inspired, and success achieved."

~ Helen Keller ~

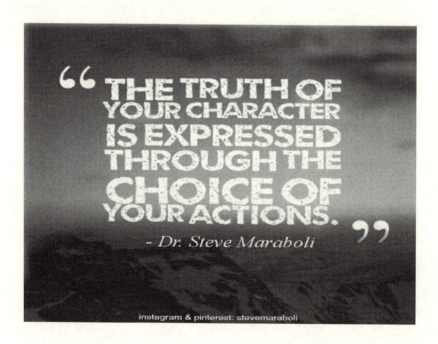

STEPS 6 & 7: WORKSHEET

"The real question is whether we can learn anything from our experiences upon which we may grow and help others to grow in the likeness and image of God. We know that if we rebel against doing that which is reasonably possible for us, then we will be penalized. And we will be equally penalized if we presume in ourselves a perfection that simply is not there. Apparently, the course of relative humility and progress will have to lie somewhere between these extremes. In our slow progress away from rebellion, true perfection is doubtless several millennia away."

~ Bill W. ~

What follows is a list of possible defects of character some of which you may be familiar with along with what represents the opposite, more positive behavior. Check to mark all those characteristics in each column that you honestly know apply to you today. In each pairing ask yourself which choice is currently more common or more relevant to your life today.

Add any other sets of contrasting behaviors that you are aware of. As time goes on, refer to this list regularly to help keep you on the positive track. Ask for God's help in all cases. Be specific in your prayer requests concerning this matter of shortcomings.

Suggestion: About a year from now, review this list and see if you notice any changes in the total checks on the two columns. If you are persistent in your work here you may well be amazed. Please do be as diligent as you can and God is sure to bless you.

SELF PITY	A GRATEFUL HEART
SUSPICIOUS	TRUST; HAVE FAITH
SELF CENTRED	THINK OF OTHERS
SELF IMPORTANT (BIG SHOT)	HUMILITY; WILLING TO LISTEN AND LEARN
IMPATIENT	ACCEPTANCE
DISHONESTY	INTEGRITY
INTOLERANCE	PATIENCE/ RESPECT FOR OTHERS
GUILT; SELF HATE	VIRTUOUSNESS
SELF CONDEMNATION	APPROBATION
WISHFUL THINKING	AUTHENTICITY
NEGATIVE THINKING	USEFUL THINKING
INDECISIVE	DETERMINED
TRASHY THINKING	HEALTHY THINKING
CRITICAL/JEALOUS OF OTHERS	TOLERANCE/ ACCEPTANCE
MENTAL/PHYSICAL LAZINESS	VIGOROUS/ DYNAMIC
PUTTING THINGS OFF	PROMPTNESS/BE ACTIVE
UNRELIABLE	THOUGHTFUL/THOROUGH
GLOOMY/POOR ME	JOYFUL/POSITIVE
AIMLESS/INDIFFERENT	FOCUSED/INVOLVED
PRONE TO WORRY	SURRENDER/ACCEPTANCE
LACK OF EMPATHY FOR OTHERS	COMPASSION/UNDERSTANDING
STUBBORN/PIG HEADED	LISTEN TO OTHERS/ADMIT MISTAKES
ANXIOUS/JITTERY/FEARFUL	PRACTICE PRAYER AND MEDITATION REGULARLY
RESENTFUL	ACCEPTING/TOLERANT
IMPATIENT	SERENE/UNDERSTANDING
GOSSIPER	LOYALTY/TRUSTWORTHY
PESSIMISTIC	HOPEFUL/EXPECTANT
BEING A TAKER	BEING A GIVER/CONTRIBUTOR

UNREALISTIC	PRACTICAL/LEVELHEADED
WHAT CAN I GET	WHAT CAN I GIVE/CONTRIBUTE
PROCRASTINATE	LIVELY/EFFECTIVE
SHY/INTROVERT	FRIENDLY/OPEN
DOMINEERING	HUMBLE/RECEPTIVE
STUBBORN	AMENABLE/FLEXIBLE
SELF DEPRECATING	SELF ESTEEM/ACCEPTANCE
SELF RIGHTEOUS	SELF HONESTY/TRUTHFULNESS

(Add any others that you become aware of.)

Einstein presents us with two interesting options. Never forget that because we are not omnipotent, our view of life is always limited. Our perception of life is all we have to work with. FYI: My opinion only. Today, you will find all those who claim to know "truth" either in the nuthouse or wandering aimlessly somewhere out in the weeds. They are truly the lost souls of the human race. I know this to be true because I was once one of them.

There are only two ways to live your life:
One is as though nothing is a miracle.
The other is as though everything is a miracle.

~ Albert Einstein ~

We have learned by this time that our most fundamental problem and also the source of all of our difficulties, before and after finding sobriety, has been a massively disproportionate and unhealthy focus on ourselves, our plans and our perceived needs. This selfishness drove us repeatedly into fruitless schemes and efforts to control and manipulate circumstances and people for our own misguided ends.

We have come to see that we were not only an abject failure at living successfully this way but also that this business of extreme self centredness is in fact the *"root of our living problems today."* We know this to be true whether drinking or sober and regardless of how far away from the last drink we have moved.

Our awareness of self and our need to nurture and protect ourselves from all perceived threats is part of nature's kit of survival tools instinctively built into each of us. This awareness is necessary and essential. But when our ego (self-awareness) is allowed to inflate beyond its necessary and healthy level we once again experience self-will running riot and we become yet again unreasonably fearful and anxious and our emotional time bomb is no doubt soon to explode.

Today we know that *humility* is not only the opposite of self centredness, it is without a doubt, the only antidote for this deadly condition of self-obsession coupled with fear and angst. *Humility* is "the" essential starting point for recovery from alcoholism and also the key for accessing happy and healthy living.

Warning! It is suggested by some that *humility*, like faith, is so fragile and elusive, that the moment we think we have it we have in fact lost it. If this is true, then we might as well throw in the towel right now and just give up.

PLEASE DON'T DO THAT!

The **REAL TRUTH** is that humility, like faith, can never be acquired like an Idea or even a belief, it can only be experienced when we are in the right mental and spiritual condition to recognize it and embrace it.

Our Creator asks of us only that we do our best each day to turn our will and our life over to His care and protection. We do this by using the intelligence He gave us to direct our thinking and our intentions towards consciously surrendering our ego and self-will *to our Higher Power. We do this through application of the step 3 prayer. The wording of this prayer is of course quite optional, it is the intent that counts.*

The following simple action honestly repeatedly practiced is the specific action that leads us to not only the experience of true humility but more importantly the *conscious awareness of living in the presence of our Heavenly Father's guidance and love.* In this moment of grace we experience honest meaningful faith and all is well. Therefore we must constantly practice acceptance of the uncontrollable and embrace the task of accommodating and adjusting to reality while staying true to our values and beliefs.

SURRENDER! SURRENDER! SURRENDER!

Acceptance of the things we cannot change is the definition of the above spiritual call to action echoing throughout the twelve steps of recovery. Giving up the delusion of personal control of one's life is only possible if there is a real belief and trust in a God of our own understanding. Only at this point can we honestly claim to know the meaning of true humility.

May we all grow in understanding and effectiveness as we continue our journey of uncovering, discovering and through it all, healing.

Our thoughts, of course, are never permanent. Whether they are good or bad, the most habitual thoughts, of course, are those that are repeated over and over again.

The change of bad thinking into good thinking can and will occur over time with diligent practice. What may begin as nothing more than a new idea will, with diligent practice and over time becomes new fundamental beliefs entrenched in our psyche. At this point these new and positive ideas replace the old and troublesome ones and become our *default thoughts* that will then spring into our consciousness seemingly on their own. At this point, for better or worse, we will reap the specific results of those thoughts, no more, no less.

Albert Einstein presents us with two interesting options. Never forget that because we are not omnipotent, our view of life is always limited and therefore incomplete. Our perception of life, regardless of how limited it may be, is all we have to work with.

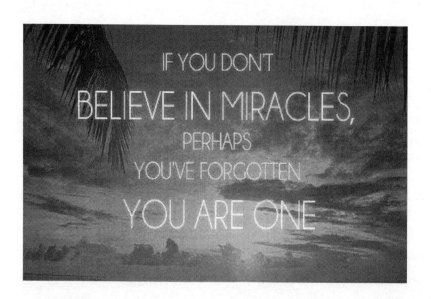

WILL I EVER GET "IT"?

Without doubt this is a question asked by almost everyone at some point in time in their pursuit of recovery through AA's twelve steps. Of course, what we are talking about is that thing called a **spiritual awakening**. That priceless moment of awareness made by the AA pioneers who wrote our book and described it so well on page 51:

"When many hundreds of people are able to say that the consciousness of the presence of God is today the most important fact of their lives, they present a powerful reason why one should have faith".

The unanswered question here is not why someone should have faith but rather: How can I acquire that kind of faith? Based on our own experience the answer to this question must be: There can be no guarantees! It will depend on ourselves and what we are prepared to do about it!

In appendix II "Spiritual Experience" page 567 of our Big Book we are told that *"Willingness, honesty and open mindedness are the indispensable essentials of recovery."*

Here we are told one more time that if we expect to ever experience faith in our Higher Power we must first practice faith by purposefully surrendering our self-will and self-management to a trust in a God of our own understanding.

Yes; it is true that in the beginning this trust is tentative and timid, but this is how we make our start into living with real faith. The fact is that most of us will find our personal spiritual awakening through a process called by William James "the educational experience" by which our faith develops slowly, through practice, over time.

Also from appendix II, *"Most of us think that this awareness of a Power Greater than ourselves is the essence of a spiritual experience. Our more religious members call it God-consciousness."*

The awareness of our higher power occurs when we actually notice God's hand at work in our daily affairs. Such incidences are usually defined as miracles or *synchronicity* as Carl Jung referred to them. Some small, some large, all are important and positively impactful to our psyche.

We are now ready to move forward if we can agree on the following assumption. "If I feel separated or distanced from my Creator, it is probably not the Creator that moved but most likely that I have created my own self centred ego driven barriers:" Let us hear from an AA member who eventually found a personal answer to this nagging question of will I ever get it.

"I spent the first two years or so of my sobriety in AA doing mainly 2 things. First, because of fear and the encouragement of my new friends, I worked the 12 steps with my sponsor and also with my group at Sunday morning step meetings a total of four times with some significant diligence. Second, during this same time I worried constantly about whether or not I might ever get "IT", that thing so many in the group obviously had and that I did not.

At the end of the above mentioned two years, one Sunday morning I listened to a reader recite from step twelve, "Having had a spiritual awakening as the result of these steps........," At this very point, I was suddenly jolted with a powerful new awareness, that totally dominated my attention and unlike anything I had experienced before. This awareness was the unshakeable conviction that whatever a spiritual awakening or experience is, "IT IS NOW MINE!" This thought was immediately followed by the statement in the Big Book, "We believe that God's will for all of us is to be happy, joyous and free.

Even though I still cannot explain or describe in words what "IT" really is, many years have passed and I have held on for dear life to this most personal and explosively enlightening moment of grace. More recently I have come to understand that this precious blessing was one of my earliest conscious moments of experiencing faith in my entire life. I suspect that this was the moment that I first let go of control and allowed my ego to take a back seat if only temporarily."

This man went on to say that he believes his original separation from this Power was probably because he felt he was not worthy of consideration by any Higher Power he could imagine and therefore needed to demonstrate to himself (probably not to God) that by working the 12 steps, he was in fact worthy of his Creators Grace.

Furthermore, he has become totally convinced that behind his extreme selfishness and self-centeredness had always been fear. Fear based on the delusion that personal success and acceptance by his peers was dependent on how well he managed his affairs, combined with the realization that he had proven himself totally inadequate to the task. He added that his overriding fear was of being found out for being the abject failure in the business of living which so many others around him were obviously very successful with. He then went to say:
"By actively and honestly working through the process of doing steps 4 through 9;(in my case it took multiple times),

I was able to make myself open to eventually experiencing the conscious awareness of the presence of God" in my own life. Since then I have come to see that it is my responsibility every day of the rest of my life to consciously practice steps 10 through 12 every day and thus grow in confidence and in reliance on His guidance."

If we haven't done so already, can we now start to break down our self-inflicted barriers and begin to experience our Creator's presence in the form of the feeling of wellbeing, happiness and purpose and to then joyfully begin practicing these new found principles in all of our affairs.

A Moment of Bliss

The Trinity in Holy Communion

To want to believe in God is the essential requirement for a ***spiritual beginning***.

To actually form a belief in God is ultimately a decision of the mind and is a ***spiritual awakening***.

However, the true goal is to know the presence of God, personally and intimately within us. This can only originate in the soul and is commonly called a ***spiritual experience***.

A *spiritual experience* is essential, not only for long term addictions recovery, but is truly the key to real wellness and peace of mind. We state this believe that we are all born with an inherent longing for this *awareness of the presence of the omnipotent.*

When untreated, we only knew this hunger as a vague craving of something undefinable and seemingly soothed only through compulsive and addictive behaviors.

In recovery we open ourselves to consciously ***knowing God's presence*** and only then will true peace become a reality.

THE SEARCH FOR OUR PERSONAL IDENTITY
(One Alcoholics Story)

You are asking yourself, as all of us must: "Who am I?"... "Where am I?"... "Whence do I go?" ... The process of enlightenment is usually slow. But, in the end, our seeking always brings a finding. These great mysteries are, after all, enshrined in complete simplicity.

~ Bill W. ~

As Bill wrote above, "who am I?" without a doubt, is one of the more universal questions asked every day by most human beings, alcoholic or not. Having now lived through more than seven decades of our own journey, I have had time to reflect on this question and maybe more importantly, to reflect on the evolution of my answer as to whom I am, as it has evolved over the course of time.

To begin with, let me give you a quick overview of the history of this question in regards to my personal journey. I, fortunately, started life with an absolute certainty as to who I was: However, from adolescence on I lived through the next 80% of my life in much doubt, uncertainty and yes sometimes despair about my perceived identity, purpose and/or relevance. Some days were better than others in terms of my opinion. Any concept of self was at best incomplete, tentative and seemingly in constant flux.

Fortunately for me, in more recent years, I am pleased and humbled to report that once again I most gratefully do enjoy a high level of certainty in my understanding of self that is quite literally a gift beyond my wildest expectations. In truth, I dare to say to you that I no longer *believe* who I am. Today I *know my true* identity for certain and that this knowledge is a priceless gift.

Before I get into the personal details of my experience I want to share with you information that comes to us through professionals who, through the work they do, have acquired some significant understanding of the human psyche and how it works. From these sources we have come to learn that for each and every one of us, there are three fundamental states or conditions that must be satisfied or fulfilled for us to be able to enjoy true wellbeing and peace of mind. These three conditions in no particular order are:

1. Personal *safety*; which includes physical, emotional and psychological safety.
2. Being of *significance* and/or value; as perceived by both self and significant others.
3. Being *situated* purposefully and therefore useful; most importantly as seen by self.

For any one of us who has worked the 12 steps, particularly step 4, with some significant effort, we can no doubt relate to experiencing these three conditions when they have not been properly addressed. The resulting discomfort was the very real cause of our resentments, fears and anxieties that would always inevitably manifest themselves. Today, as a natural corollary, we can also see that these three essential conditions when properly fulfilled are essential to being able to enjoy any real personal peace of mind and true mental health.

For many of us, as a young child; and because our home life was such that we certainly felt safe, we knew that we were loved and certainly felt that we belonged. Our security was comfortably intact. Our definable identity at that time required no more than the fact that we were the children of our mother and father and the brother or sister of our siblings and therefore we were a natural and integral member the family. To put it most clearly, in the simplicity of the juvenile mind, our needs were being fully addressed. Today, we also realize that we were most blessed to have been part of a not too dysfunctional family and that not everyone was as well situated or cared for as we were. There is no doubt about it, as a child, personal *security; significance* and *purpose* were not at issue in our case.

In time, with the onset of adolescence, our instincts and circumstances forced us to begin to move outside of our comfortable childhood bubble. That is when those erstwhile dark companions of insecurity, uncertainty and in due course self disappointment began to raise their ugly head. Fear of failure became more and more common. Lack of confidence became more and more the norm. Eventually fear of being found out as a fraud and not measuring up in the eyes of others was truly a reality. To cover up, lying and deceit was the only resource known to us for a very long time. These conditions remained and grew within us well into our biological adult life. It seems that emotionally and psychologically our development stalled and we remained a child in an adult world and suffered the obvious consequences. Sadly, our only excuse is that at the time we did not know any better.

Throughout the next many years, we remained uncomfortable, insecure and inadequate in most of life's situations. Wanting desperately to fit in, the only solution available to us to ease the pain of living was to take a few drinks which, as you well know, became a problem of overwhelming proportions.

Because we felt so negative about exactly who we were, it is obvious to us today that the cause of our discomfort was that the three essential conditions for wellbeing described earlier, were not being effectively met. Although we did not know it at the time, it was not our negative feelings that were the problem. The problem was the presence of these three unfulfilled conditions or requirements for wellness, *security, significance* and situation. The self-deprecation was just the consequences or symptoms of the real problem.

All we can say is thank Heaven for AA's Twelve Steps! Little did we know when we first arrived at what a huge blessing was in store for us by simply opting for the healing made available through personally addressing these now proven 12 steps. Not only did the personal application of these steps solve our drink problem, but equally importantly, it solved our living problems and also by necessity addressed our personal identity problem.

Because our drinking problem and living problems are dealt with in detail elsewhere in this journal, we want to focus specifically on our identity problem and the ultimate solution offered.

As the result of much work on the 12 steps, and the passage of a great deal of time, we have arrived at a stage in our life, once again, in which we know without a doubt just who we really are. Unlike our childhood experience however, this time our understanding is much deeper, more secure and more meaningful. This is because the self-identity we embrace today is most powerful and meaningful and totally satisfies those three requirements of *safety, significance* and *purpose* discussed earlier. Now, let me tell you who we really are. (By the way, and by necessity, I also know who you really are as well.) What follows is a direct product of investing totally in the power of the twelve steps to heal and grow. No more and no less than that.

Today we know, beyond the shadow of any doubt, that we are most definitely not the result of some sort of universal accident or chance event, but rather the direct product of a loving creator and as a consequence endowed with both significance and purpose. Most simply stated, we are just as you are: One of God's kids. Some may choose to call themselves children of the universe or simply a part or piece of creation. We think all are equally valid and simply a matter of personal preference. How we perceive our connection to the Great Reality is of no great concern. Knowing that we are an integral part of all that is rather than being separated from the Great Reality is the key here.

Our journey to this point began many years ago when we first made the decision that from that point on, as far as we were concerned, we bought in 100% to the option offered on page 53 of the Big Book that *"God is: God is everything: and therefore must include me"*. Acceptance of that idea did, in short order, bring us from a state of separateness and loneliness into a state of unity, wholeness and completeness for the first time in our life.

With that honest, humble and tentative beginning, an ever growing faith in the *Great Reality* and our connection to it makes it impossible for us to not feel secure in all that we are regardless of circumstance. There is no need for fear anymore because *"wherever we go: He goes"*. We dare not and want not to separate ourselves from our Source. We also have a healthy feeling of significance and value because we know today, without a doubt, that you, just like us, are truly a product of God's creation and that God does not make mistakes. We belong here. We, just like you, are of significance. We have a purpose, and that purpose most simply stated, is to be the best example of being one of God's kids that we can possibly be.

Finally we are situated and purposeful because we know without a doubt that as we go through our day, God will always show us what the next right thing to do is and if we ask, He will always give us the courage to carry that out.

Therefore, let us not spend one more second of time trapped in our self-created misery and isolation and open our minds and hearts to God's universal love and care and find our way into that little bit of heaven available to us right here on earth, right now. You have suffered for far too long.

> **Nobody can teach me who I am. You can describe parts of me, but who I am and what I need is something I have to find out myself.**

STEPS EIGHT AND NINE

(8) Made a list of all persons we had harmed, and became willing to make amends to them all. (9) Made direct amends to such people wherever possible except when to do so would injure them or others.

"I try hard to hold fast to the truth that a full and thankful heart cannot entertain great conceits. When brimming with gratitude, one's heartbeat must surely result in outgoing love, the finest emotion we can ever know."

~ Bill W~

THE LETTER

My Beloved Child

How are you? I just had to send a note to tell you how much I care about you. I saw you yesterday as you were talking with your friends. I waited all day hoping you would want to talk to me too. I gave you a sunset to close your day and a cool breeze to rest you – and I waited. You never came. It hurt me, but I still love you because you are my friend. I saw you sleeping last night and longed to touch your brow, so I spilled moonlight upon your face. Again I waited, wanting to rush down so we could talk.

I have so many gifts for you! But you awoke and rushed off to work. My tears were in the rain.

If you would only listen to me! I love you! I try to tell you in the blue skies and in the quiet green grasses and in the leaves on the trees and I breathe it into the colours of the flowers; I shout it to you in mountain streams and give the birds songs to sing.

My love for you is deeper than the ocean, and bigger than the greatest need in your heart! Ask me! Talk to me! I have so much to share with you! I won't hassle you any further. It is you I have chosen and for you I will wait.

Please don't forget me.
Your Eternal and Loving Creator

Now at steps eight and nine, we are asked to go about the business of addressing the damage we have done to those people negatively affected by our alcoholic behaviors in the past. Amends are of two types; direct amends and living amends. At this point, our focus is to be on direct amends. Living amends will be addressed in steps ten through twelve later when we address the often called maintenance steps (10 to 12) or as we prefer to call them *"the living and/or growth steps."*

From our step four we have a readymade list of amends to make. But first, let's answer two operative questions you might have at this point.

(a) *Am I really prepared to go through with this undoubtedly very humbling experience or not?* (If in doubt, be true to yourself and talk it over with your sponsor.)

(b) *How, exactly, should each required amend be done?* (You will want to consult with your sponsor about the specifics of this second question. Consultation is very important to making sure we get the job done properly.)

"We lose the fear of making decisions, great and small; as we realize that should our choice prove wrong we can, if we will, learn from the experience."

~Bill W~

Now, with your amends list at the ready, please consider the following questions; after which your honest answers will clearly tell you what your next course of action must be.

STEPS 8 & 9: WORKSHEET

1. Do I honestly recognize that there are people in my past that I have harmed and in fact deserve my redress?

        Yes ☐   No ☐   Not Sure ☐

2. Can I say truthfully that I know taking the suggested actions here is vital for my long term recovery?

        Yes ☐   No ☐   Not Sure ☐

3. In approaching these people, can I ignore any perceived or real fault on their part and address only my side of the issue?

        Yes ☐   No ☐   Not Sure ☐

4. If I owe money, am I prepared to make workable arrangements with the lender to re-pay the debt?

        Yes ☐   No ☐   Not Sure ☐

5. If the answer is yes to the previous question will I make it an essential priority to follow through?

        Yes ☐   No ☐   Not Sure ☐

6. Can I avoid expressing any criticism towards the other person?

        Yes ☐   No ☐   Not Sure ☐

7. Can I apply tact and common sense in each case as to whether or not I introduce the topic of the role of God in my current actions?

        Yes ☐   No ☐   Not Sure ☐

8. If someone rebukes my apology can I let that pass as water under the bridge and move on?

        Yes ☐   No ☐   Not Sure ☐

9. In this process, if somehow a new resentment is created in me, am I prepared immediately to address this shortcoming specifically through the step 7 prayer?
Yes ☐   No ☐   Not Sure ☐

10. Will I make every effort to make sure that I do not harm anyone else in the process of making these amends?
Yes ☐   No ☐   Not Sure ☐

11. I will make sure that when making an amend involving a third party that all appropriate protection is maintained to guard their anonymity?
Yes ☐   No ☐   Not Sure ☐

12. For wrongs that cannot be fully righted, am I prepared to keep myself in state of readiness to do so if an opportunity arises?
Yes ☐   No ☐   Not Sure ☐

13. I believe in the premise that "faith without works is dead" and therefore, I will, with my sponsor's guidance, make every reasonable effort to do my part in correcting my past mistakes. I need to do this for my sake as well as theirs?
Yes ☐   No ☐   Not Sure ☐

14. Because I am "doing the right thing", I know that now I do not do this alone. Therefore, whatever happens is as it should be and therefore good.
Yes ☐   No ☐   Not Sure ☐

Spiritual healing will begin to occur as we begin to consciously reconnect with our *"essential inner being"* - that wise, loving, powerful, creative entity that we can only find deep down within us at the true core of our being. This is the healing place within you. The healing is a gift you were granted at the moment of your creation; just as all such divine gifts were bequeathed.

Your creator calls out to you to use your gifts now. Recognize and applaud the divine beauty, the courage, the hope and the love that is in you. Call upon your new found strength of faith and trust. Use your gifts of acceptance and compassion when present with others who you can now see are your true spiritual brothers and sisters. Even during sad times joy is within you. Bring it forth. Wisdom is there to guide you. Use any one of your gifts and you will rouse the power of your healing place. Use all of them and you will endure and flourish.

When what we demand from life does not conform to what life has to offer and our kit of spiritual tools is nowhere to be found, we are in deep trouble.

~ Anonymous. ~

RECOGNIZING RECOVERY

(WHAT FOLLOWS IS WHAT WE HAVE COME TO BELIEVE IS THE STUFF OF OUR OWN RECOVERY)

Because recovery from any addiction is all about a change to one's state of mind and/or outlook on life and because recovery is totally a personal experience, the honest answer to the question of *"when will I know what recovery is"* must always be: *"You can only know it when you have it"*.

Due to the fact that new thoughts are constantly popping into one's consciousness seemingly out of nowhere, and are constantly changing and uncontrollable, it is appropriate to say that no one is ever totally cured of an addiction and/or an obsession of the mind. That is why many sober members of AA and other 12 step treated addictions insist on referring to themselves as recovering even after many years of sobriety and/or abstinence.

However, these same individuals will happily tell you that they have in fact recovered from a *"hopeless state of mind and body"* contingent upon maintaining a conscious, ongoing relationship with their personal Higher Power. For this reason they are no longer willing victims to the sometimes called "slings and arrows of life". In other words, they see themselves as participants in life no longer victims.

<u>Disclaimer</u>: Those of us who write this guide would like to share with you what we discovered when we experienced our own moments of conscious awakening to the presence of the Grace of recovery in our own lives: And because every individual's case is different please take this information or leave it as you see fit. What follows is

nothing more than our own interpretation of our own experience. Also, we recognize and readily admit that our words here are hopelessly incomplete and inadequate to explain the unknowable. That being said, what follows is what we are compelled to share with those of you who may be interested.

We have found that when we honestly take the time through prayer and meditation to get connected with Our Creator and totally surrender our will and our life into His care, the following five realities/feelings of (1)humility, (2)surrender/acceptance, (3)faith/trust, (4)peace of mind and finally (5)gratitude always come to dominate our consciousness during those moments. Each one of these realities seems to be inter-connected and interactive with the others. They transition rapidly into and out of our consciousness one overlapping with the next and for that incredible moment in time they combine to create a state of awareness that in the simplest terms possible we can best describe as:

"We truly feel as one with the Great Reality and that for this one blessed moment, there is not a single thing of importance lacking in our own reality. We are totally satiated and completely empty of self"

*Is there anything more splendid than this that a once hopeless, helpless lost soul could possibly ask for? Many of us consider these particular moments of grace to be the spiritual **"returning home"** that as lost untreated victims of our disease we experienced as nothing more than a persistent but vague craving. By continuing the practice of putting the principles of recovery to work in our lives, we are learning that we are spending more and more of our day **"spiritually at home"**. What a priceless blessing! These moments are always fleeting and elusive and leave us forever craving the next such sublime experience.*

Recovery is based on the belief that it can only be found through experiencing these moments of personal unity with that power greater than ourselves that we are just now awakening to. We suspect that this power is universal as well as personal. It seems that a personal connection to this Higher Power, regardless of how we may interpret it, is in fact the vital force that permits us to recognize and appreciate the reality of the true unity that exists in the universe and that forever binds us all together in true oneness.

Can we now begin to divest ourselves of our selfish and limiting ego that demands that we align ourselves separately from and different from all others. Ultimately, recovery is not just something cognitive, it is something totally experiential. It is not imagined: It is something we feel and is very, very real. Its source is not in our head but somewhere deep down within our innermost self where our true or real self can only ever be found.

We pursue the twelve steps not to understand recovery but instead to open ourselves to the receiving of the priceless gift of the recovery experience which is something much more real than the recovery idea. Recovery is totally experiential and involves expression from our innermost self and is obviously far beyond a merely human thought or idea.

Once recovery is experienced, its anticipated return will be the source of a new craving that will be with us for the rest of our life. That obsession is a positive one and will be the persistent desire to spend as much of our life as possible in the presence of this priceless gift of unity and oneness with the Divine Creator ultimately to be found only in that special place deep down inside of ourselves where only the truth can be found.

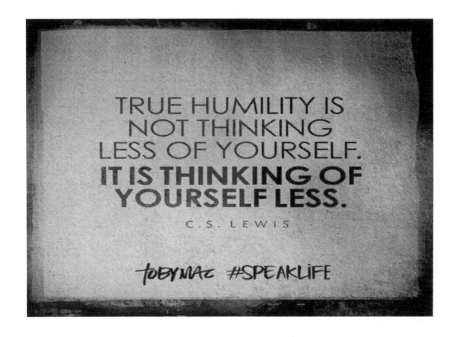

"If you wish to experience peace, provide peace for another. If you wish to know that you are safe, cause another to know that they are safe. If you wish to better understand seemingly incomprehensible things, help others to better understand you. If you wish to heal your own sadness or anger, seek to heal the sadness or anger of another."

~ The Dalai Lama ~

Let us now have a look at one man's interpretation/model of his own recovery experience.

THE FIVE REALITIES OF RECOVERY

HUMILITY → "I need help"
                              becomes **SURRENDER**
SURRENDER → "Asking for help"
                              becomes **FAITH**
FAITH → "Trust that we are getting that help"
                              becomes **PEACE**
PEACE → Being without pain or need
                              becomes **GRATITUDE**
GRATITUDE → Thankfulness
                              becomes **HUMILITY**

As you can see in this model, humility is the alpha and the omega: The beginning and the end of a personal recovery experience. Without humility we will continue to be trapped in our self-directed misery and forever be on the outside of life looking in.

However, with humility, regardless of circumstances, we will inevitably come to know that not only are we exactly who we are supposed to be; we are also precisely where we should be at any moment in time and in fact doing specifically what it is we are supposed to be doing. We will intuitively know that we are on the inside of life now and not on the outside looking in as was the old norm. Now on the inside and maybe for the first time ever we become aware that we are an integral and useful part of humanity. We will be at peace because we will know that we now have access to that essential *"Perfect Power"* that is the essential ingredient required to live a wellness filled life.

Yes, it is true that initially in step one, most of us first experienced humiliation and not humility. This is because our ego (which at that time was still dominating our thinking) was vulnerable and hurt. Humiliation is of those children spawned by the ego. Humiliation is of course a very unnatural and diseased state of being we are all too familiar with. At this early stage of our recovery we must let the group and our new found friends carry us forward. We will grow away from humiliation into humility through working the twelve steps

Later, after properly addressing steps two, three and four, we will go ahead with step five because we are now experiencing some small degree of true humility. By this time we have acquired just enough faith to suppress our ego for the moment and as well, we carry with us the real hope that admitting our failures to another human being just may become a door opener into healing and eventually a new and more successful way of life. It is at this point that we will be consciously practicing some real faith (trust) that we are doing the right thing and therefore all will be well.

From this point on, when we choose to pick up our spiritual tools and apply them, we begin to **experience** real recovery. Our consciousness becomes filled with the previously noted five realities. At this blessed moment, peace of mind crowds out all selfish concerns and desires and once again we discover that there is not a single thing in the world worth having that we do not already possess. Again, I ask you, my brothers and sisters: *What more could anyone of God's children ever possibly ask for?*

GOD'S GRACE
(The blessings of unanswered prayers)

I asked for strength, that I might achieve;
I was made weak, that I might learn humbly to obey.

I asked for health, that I might do better things;
I was given infirmity, that I might do greater things.

I asked for riches, that I might be happy;
I was given poverty, that I might be wise.

I asked for power, that I might have the praise of men;
I was given weakness, that I might feel the need of God.

I asked for all these things, that I might enjoy life;
I was given life, that I might enjoy all things.

I got nothing I asked for but everything I had hope for.
Almost despite myself, my unspoken prayers were answered.

I, among all men, am most richly blessed.

(Found in the possession of a fallen confederate soldier, 1863)

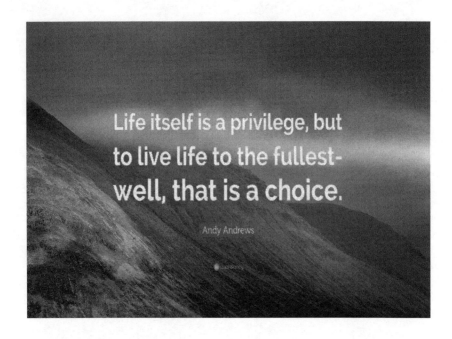

PART II: LIVING AND GROWING IN RECOVERY
(Steps Ten to Twelve)

This is the part of the program that we are asked to practice for each and every day of the rest of our life. As suggested by Doctor Bob: Let's try and keep it simple.

STEP TEN

Continued to take personal inventory and when we were wrong promptly admitted it

For the wise have always known that no one can make much of his life until self-searching has become a regular habit, until he is able to admit and accept what he finds, and until he patiently and persistently tries to correct what is wrong.

~Bill W. ~

Hopefully, by this point in our journey we have fulfilled the conditions of the first nine steps, at least to the point of discovering for ourselves that we have gained some measure of sobriety. As well, some, if not all of the promises offered to us on pages 83 and 84 of our **Big Book**, have and are now making, at least brief appearances in our life. If that be the case then we are now ready to look closely at these so-called maintenance steps that we the writers prefer to call the *"daily living"* or *"growth"* steps.

Note: *If however, if those promises remain wishful thinking and sobriety remains elusive, re-visiting steps one to nine in a timely manner would be highly recommended. Putting the cart before the horse will gain us nothing.*

By continuing to address these last three steps on a daily basis we can be assured that we are doing what is necessary to maintain our sobriety and continue the life-long business of growing in understanding and effectiveness, which the AA pioneers who wrote our book promise us is to be our happy destiny.

It will take a real personal commitment each and every day to take time for meditation and prayer not just in the morning and at night but also throughout the day whenever emotional disturbances occur and situations warrant. Because each new day is a new spiritual start, we need to do this constantly to re-establish a renewed conscious awareness and connection to our Creator. At these times we ask only for His guidance, His strength and His love along with the power to carry out His will as best as we can. We make these prayerful requests with honest humility because by now we know all too well the futility of trying to go it alone. We know that it is only through the Grace of our Heavenly Father that we can even hope to become a better example of trying to be a righteous child of the universe. This is what we believe is to be our true destiny in this life.

To do this, we must begin to practice putting some self-discipline and serious consideration into not only our thought selection but also our choice of words and actions. This is how we grow in understanding and effectiveness.

To be sure, the real challenge with these steps is not when life is a struggle but rather when living is easy. It is at these particular moments that we can be inclined to relax on our commitment a little and if not to completely forget to take the prescribed actions we may begin to procrastinate and apply some not so good short cuts. This is when our precious sobriety not only becomes at risk, but also life itself begins to lose some of its lustre and we soon fall back into that not so good "grey zone" of living that the Big Book correctly describes as being dull, boring and glum. Based on our own observations through the course of our own journeys we suspect that some non-drinking AA members stay that way for the rest of their life. May God grant that it not be us!

Our book gives us very specific suggestions of what we can do in working these three steps. Ultimately, each of us will make our own choices about how and when we will address them and that is exactly how it should be: But keeping in mind the following truth:

"Every positive or negative event in your life was attracted to you. Positive thoughts and behaviors attract only positive results."

~source unknown~

OUR TRUE HOME

Our true home is the present moment.
To live in the present moment is a miracle.
The miracle is not to walk on water,
the miracle is to walk on the green earth
in the present moment:
And to appreciate the peace and beauty
that is available now.
Peace is all around us- in the world and in nature-
and within us- in our bodies and spirit.
Once we learn to touch this peace,
we will be healed and transformed.
It is a matter of faith; it is a matter of practice.

~Source Unknown~

The peace within us as noted in the above prayer can be more specifically defined as peace of mind. For many of us, the essence of peace of mind is the all-consuming awareness that when present and for that very real moment in time, not only do we experience true wellbeing but we are also blessedly conscious of the fact that there is not a single thing of importance lacking in our lives.

Although we would not have realized it at the time, many of us first began to look for this ever elusive peace of mind through the bottom of a bottle or glass of alcohol. It was only later that we discovered that the "peace" alcohol had to offer was a disappointingly shallow fraud of the real thing. Much later, through applying ourselves honestly to the 12 steps, we come to discover the grace of true and lasting peace of mind.

"How we choose to perceive the world we live in is the single most important factor in ultimately determining the level of happiness we will allow ourselves to experience."

~ Wayne Dyer ~

Ultimately, our personal well-being has little or nothing to do with our surroundings but everything to do with what we allow to dominate our consciousness. The events of life are of themselves neither good nor bad. It is how we interpret these events that is the real issue. The fact is we are definitely not as helpless and hopeless with regards to the so called slings and arrows of life as we naively once thought. Please consider the following statement carefully.

The world we human beings inhabit here on earth is surely an integral and vital part of God's universe. But make no mistake; this earthly world is not as it is because God willed it. This world of ours is strictly of our own making.

I would like to suggest that just as a sandbox is the domain of little children for learning how to socialize and get along with each other, this planet of ours is really a humanities sandbox, created by God, for us to learn how to use our self-will appropriately. That means how to get along peacefully and positively. It is obvious that we are not there yet!

The undeniable reality is that we live and function in an often chaotic, dysfunctional and noisy, humanity driven world more often than not propelled by power hungry self-seekers fueled by misunderstanding and fear. As the result, that peace of mind we associate with recovery will always be transient at best. However, with practice, we can become more and more efficient at accessing this peace by using our spiritual tools. In so doing we strengthen and sustain our conscious awareness of our creator as we understand Him. This truth is one of the most important realities about recovery that we need to embrace.

At this point let's take a minute to listen to what an AA old-timer told us he discovered for himself about his own recovery journey.

"After 25 years of sobriety of which the last 15 years or so found me submerged in something less than good sober living I prefer to refer to as a *"grey zone"*, three thoughts gradually came into focus and, over time, became operative for me:

FIRST: That the Big Book teaches us that half measures avail us nothing. It appears that a commitment to finding and maintaining a faith in a power greater than ourselves is something like being pregnant: You cannot have some of it, it is all or nothing! *What was my choice to be?*

SECOND: The Law of Attraction states; *"life can only give back to us what we give to it."* This tells me that the quality and quantity of energy put into my thoughts and actions will be clearly evident in how life is coming back at me. More simply, positive energy output can attract only positive energy in return. *How am I thinking and acting today?*

THIRD: Something a wise old AA long-timer told me a long time ago.

> *Son, don't sell your-self short with respect to spiritual growth. God loves all of us as only He can; with Infinite Love. That's all He can do because He is love and that's all the love there is.*

Our problem is ourselves and our own sick ego driven inability to surrender completely to Him and accept without reservation and without question, His love in its entirety and to then share that love immediately with others. The only way we can keep His love is to give it away.

So do yourself a favour and do what you have to do to get as close to Him as you possibly can to get all of that "good loving" that you possibly can right here and now and start enjoying living as He wants you to.

The infectious aura of peace and wellbeing emanating from this man made it impossible for me to ignore his words even if I might have wanted to. Consequently, I have totally bought into these three premises. Today I know that, at least for me, these three suppositions are true. My hope and prayer for you is that you won't be as slow as I to pick up on them. If we cannot find a little bit of heaven right here on earth right now, then we have no one to blame but ourselves.

The purpose of the AA fellowship is to provide friendship, support and guidance. The purpose of the AA twelve steps is to provide a pathway to finding personal recovery by finding a faith in a personal higher power

MY MEDALLION

I always carry my medallion. It is a simple reminder to me
of the fact that I'm in recovery no matter where I may be.
This small chip is not magic nor is it a good luck charm.
It isn't supposed to protect me from all possible harm.

It is not meant for comparison, or for everyone to see.
It is simply an understanding between my Higher Power and me.

It reminds me to be grateful When doubt and worry smothers me. To take the time to remember Just how hopeless it used to be.

It reminds me to be thankful for my blessings day by day.
And to practice all the principles in everything I do and say.

It is also a daily reminder of the peace and comfort I share
With all who work the program and show they really care.

So I carry my medallion to remind no one but me
That the promises will unfold if I let God work for me.

~Adapted from the poem by the same name~

We can easily manage if each day, we only take up the burden appointed to it. The load will be too heavy for us if we carry yesterday's burden over again today and then add the burden of tomorrow before we are required to bear it.
~ John Newton ~

GIVERS AND TAKERS

Let us take a minute to reflect on our own efforts to date in regards to walking the walk of recovery. Are we givers or takers? Or, more likely, are we somewhere in between these two extremes? Honest personal appraisal done without remorse or self-denigration always needs to be a part of our ongoing application of step ten.

Alcoholics Anonymous as an institution consists of two parts. It incorporates both a fellowship component and a recovery program. Participating in both parts makes for a healthy happy recovery. The fellowship and the recovery program are intimately intertwined and interdependent but are actually two very different things.

As important and helpful as it is, attending meetings and even sharing at meetings is solely a part of experiencing the AA fellowship and along with providing ongoing hope, it helps to expand and grow our relationship with like-minded individuals in a positive way. However, this form of social growth, of itself, is not capable of generating the essential *"psychic change"* required for personal recovery. Recovery demands personally taking the actions clearly offered in the twelve steps as spelled out in our Big Book. This takes help. This is where a good sponsor along with a dynamic and ongoing personal commitment to participating in the AA fellowship will make sobriety actually become a reality.

When we are new to AA, we attend meetings because we have to. We are told that we must in order to entertain any thought of staying sober. When we walk into the meeting room as a newcomer our interest, out of necessity, is about what we might be able to get out of the meeting to come. This is to be expected because as newcomers, a little hope is likely the most that any of us can muster at this point.

As time passes and our work on the 12 steps continues, we will grow in our recovery. At some point we will know that positive changes are taking place within us because we happily discover that our expectations towards our meetings have in fact changed. At this point we find ourselves going to meetings not to try to get something.

Now we find that we are more interested in what we can add to the meeting at hand rather than what we might get out of it. At the same time we discover that we are now going to the meetings because we want to be there rather than because we have to. These are vital and important personal discoveries.

We find that we have in fact grown from being focused totally inwards on ourselves and our needs to a more healthy looking outwards towards others. Many of you reading this will be saying to yourself "Yes! I know that to be true in my own experience." Hang on to this knowledge brothers and sisters. This discovery is important. This is a true indicator of your own growth in your own recovery.

However, if it be the case that by the time of our first sober AA anniversary you have not yet experienced this change, it would be a reasonable assumption that even though you may have been busy at participating in the fellowship of alcoholics anonymous, you have been "short changing" yourself in respect to the recovery part of the program. You may well want to re-evaluate how you are working the 12 step program.

Finally; for those of us looking forward with hope and anticipation to celebrating our first full year of sobriety and to those of us who have already reached this important milestone, we certainly can and should allow ourselves to enjoy a moment of real achievement. It is a big deal! However, to be realistic, we must combine that sense of achievement with an honest sense of gratitude to those that helped us on the way and most importantly to The God of our own understanding. Without question, we do not arrive at this point on our own.

> *"In the midst of winter, I found there was, within me, an invincible summer. And that makes me happy. For it says that no matter how hard the world pushes against me, within me, there's something stronger — something better, pushing right back."*
>
> ~Albert Camus~

SOME FOOD FOR THOUGHT

God is a true gentleman/lady. He / She will never arrive without an invitation.

I am never in control of what happens around me, but I am always in control of what happens within me.

Doing what you like may be called freedom, but liking what you do is most certainly happiness.

To believe there is a God is a product of the mind and may be considered a spiritual awakening. To know that there is a God is a product of the heart and can only be called a spiritual experience.

"Once you become aware that the main business that you are here for is to know God, most of life's problems fall into place of their own accord.

"The issue is fear. But the deeper issue is trust. Can we trust our lives, our futures, and the lives of those we love to God? Can we trust a God we can't control? Can we trust this God whose take on life and death and suffering and joy is so very different from our own? Yes. Yes, we can: Because deep down within us, we know him. And we know he is good."

It is not happiness that leads to gratitude. Rather, it is gratitude that leads to happiness.

The author of the following poem tells us that the origin of this creative effort came during a period of personal neglect and lethargy concerning working his daily program. Fortunately his sponsor soon noticed and nudged him to do A little serious "self" evaluation and hopefully become a little more helpful and agreeable to be around. Once again a good sponsor proves to be a priceless blessing.

THIS DAY

*Every passing day I get a little older.
Each new day I move a little slower.
But to follow the way and to fulfill this day
I must give a little time to the needs of my brother
And smile a little more.*

*Each new day brings gifts that astound me.
Each new day provides the strength that sustains me
But come what may and to live this day
I must give a little time to the needs of my brother
And smile a little more.*

*With the morning sun's warmth my body is fueled.
With the morning sun's light my soul is renewed.
But still they say; to enjoy this day,
I must give a little time to the needs of my brother
And smile a little more.*

*When nightfall comes and rest is near.
When nightfall comes and memories are held dear.
May I be able to say that I lived this day,
And gave a little time to the needs of my brother
And smiled just a little more.*

~ Anonymous~

STEP ELEVEN

We sought through prayer and meditation to improve our conscious contact with God as we understood Him, praying only for knowledge of His will for us and the power to carry that out.

"Is sobriety all that we are to expect of a spiritual awakening? No, sobriety is only a bare beginning; it is only the first gift of the first awakening. If more gifts are to be received, our awakening has to go on. As it does go on, we find that bit by bit we can discard the old life - the one that did not work - for a new life that can and does work under any conditions.

~ Bill W~

The following are some suggestions for the application of the "daily living" or "growth" steps, #10, 11 and 12.

Never forget that regardless of the number of days of sobriety we may have accrued, our recovery still only begins upon awakening to each new day. Yesterday provides us with experiences. Those experiences, good or bad, certainly can serve to be helpful going forward. More importantly, *we must consciously surrender to God's will every new day because we have not been here before!* Always remember to take the time to start the day armed and ready to practice good positive living.

#1: At the start of the day: Take the time, even if it means multi-tasking, to establish the right relationship with your Higher Power for this day. May we suggest that you remind yourself of the following three facts.

(a) When asked, God will always do for you what you cannot do for yourself. Therefore take the time to ask Him honestly and purposefully for this help and then you need not worry about at least 95% of the day ahead.

(b) As to the remaining 5% of the day; ask that in each new circumstance you be given the wisdom and courage to do the next right thing. Do this and you need not worry about the upcoming day at all.

(c) Finally, take the time to reflect long enough on the reality of your life today to experience an honest sense of gratitude for the good things in your life. This reminder will provide you with a real and meaningful state of humility that will then automatically generate a true sense of wellbeing to take with you as you walk out the door. If all else fails in this regard then reflect for a moment on what it was like before recovery.

When agitated or rushed during the day: Take a mental time out ASAP to slow down the brain by repeating the serenity prayer (mentally if necessary) or any other prayer of choice. Repeat as needed. When calm returns, thank God for being with you. Ask for guidance to deal with the immediate situation properly. Most importantly remind yourself that you are not alone. *"God is! God is in you; as you; is you! Wherever you go God goes".* Proceed with your business confident in the knowledge that you are getting the required direction you need and that in fact you are not only exactly who you are supposed to be, but you are also precisely where you are supposed to be, and no doubt you are doing specifically what it is you are supposed to be doing for this moment in time. Do this and you will know that all is well!

#3: At or near the end of the day: Give thanks to your Higher Power for another day of sobriety; the best gift any alcoholic can possibly hope for. Review your day and ask to be made aware of any amends that need to be made and if so, resolve to do so at the earliest opportunity. Do this and you will have eliminated any unnecessary mental baggage and you can now travel lightly into the new day.

#4: Stay involved: As time passes and we become healthier, it is vital that we continue to find some meaningful way to continue to help those less fortunate than ourselves. As step 12 tells us, the ongoing grace of a spiritual awakening depends on our continued willingness to give of ourselves through acts of service and to do so as anonymously as possible. It is most important for our own long term wellness to never forget what Dr. Bob said about why he stayed active and involved in service to other alcoholics for the rest of his life; (from p. 181, Doctor Bob's Nightmare; The Big Book).

-A sense of duty

-It is a pleasure
-Because in so doing, I am paying my debt to the man who took the time to pass it on to me
-Because every time I do it I take out a little more insurance for myself against a possible slip.

The fellowship of AA is a shared reality. Recovery through the practice of the 12 steps is totally a personal reality

~Anonymous~

For those interested, the following is a suggestion for a morning reading. It is generally a good idea to have a variety of meaningful prayers and readings available to help keep the exercise fresh. It is important to use meditation time purposefully.

On a personal note: The following prayer was given to us by our sponsor many years ago. To this day, it can be found attached to the inside of the cover of our original copy of the Big Book. On countless occasions this message has provided us with needed comfort, strength and hope. More recently we had the great pleasure to return this same gift to our sponsor in celebration of his 40th year of sobriety. It did not escape our attention that The Law of Attraction was at work here.

I AM RESOLVED

I believe that my Brother intended that I take His teachings in the simple, frank and open manner in which He gave them, out on the hillside, by the calm blue waters of the Galilean Sea and out under the stars of heaven.

I believe that He knew what He meant, and that He meant what He said, when He gave the substance of all religion and the duty of man, as love to God, and love and service for his fellow men.

I am therefore resolved at this, the beginning of another day, this fresh beginning of life, to go forth eager and happy and unafraid, in that I can come into the same filial relations of love and guidance and care with my Father in Heaven, that my elder brother realized and lived, and going before revealed to me.

I shall listen intently to know, and shall run with eager feet to do my Father's will, calm and quiet within, knowing that I shall have the Divine guidance and care, and that no harm therefore shall befall me; for I am now living in God's life and there I shall live forever.

I am resolved in all human contact to meet petulance with patience, questionings with kindness, hatred with love; eager always to do the kindly deed that brings the joy of service – and that alone makes human life truly worth living.

I shall seek no advantage for myself to the detriment or harm of my neighbour, knowing that it is only through the law of mutuality that I can fully enjoy what I gain – or even be a man.

I am resolved therefore to live this day, that when the twilight comes and night falls, I shall be not only another day's journey nearer home, but I shall have lived a man's part and done a man's work in the world – and shall indeed merit my Father's love and care.

~Source unknown~

THE REALITY OF LIFE

To get to the core of the matter we need to know and accept the fact that life always is and will be just what it is. *Life is what it is.*

Of itself, the events of life are neither good nor bad. Good and bad are simply human descriptors or judgements made by the individual based on their own criteria or needs.

If there is a problem in one's life, the problem does not belong to life it is owned solely by the beholder.

Therefore, it is how we choose to interpret life's circumstances that truly matters. Are we in conflict with life or are we in harmony with life? That is the question.

"Perhaps one of the greatest rewards of meditation and prayer is the sense of belonging that comes to us".

~Bill W ~

The following essay addresses some questions and concerns that came to my mind about a decade ago when personal discomfort and frustration demanded my attention. Ultimately, through prayer and meditation I was guided to the personal affirmation of the two assumptions stated there in and as the result of honestly addressing the five questions posed, I was able to reaffirm my commitment to practice the 12 steps daily and also re-committed to practicing the AA plan of recovery in its entirety. The result has been an ever expanding personal world of wellbeing, love and purposefulness. I have been most truly blessed.

IS THIS AS GOOD AS IT'S EVER GOING TO GET?

Many of us who have been sober in Alcoholics Anonymous for some time can, at some point in our personal journey in recovery, certainly identify with this question. The words may be different but the concern is always the same.

Long after the glow of the pink cloud that carried us through our early recovery has passed, we may well experience a quality of life that gratefully includes sobriety but may not be as fulfilling and satisfying as we might wish. To find a definitive answer to this question can also seem to be frustratingly elusive. Maybe, this time, we can find the answer we are looking for. Let's start by considering the following two assumptions.

(a) If the quality of my life today is not what I realistically desire it to be, then I am the only one able to do anything about it.

(b) If I am not as consciously close to my Higher Power today as I would like to be, it is undoubtedly me that has moved.

If you are willing to assume that these two assumptions are true, then let us consider the following questions honestly. In the process, maybe we will be able to see where we really are in regards to practicing the AA twelve steps in our daily affairs. Before we can set a new course to a new destination we first of all must find out precisely where we are right now. Only then can we set out with a realistic chance of getting ourselves to where we want to go.

1. Did I ever really do all of the 12 steps to the best of my ability? (To "do" a step means to take specific actions. Talking about an action is not doing it.) If the answer is no, what did I omit? Am I now willing to do anything about it?

2. Even if the answer is an honest yes to the previous question, how are things going in my life right now? How much water has passed under the bridge since my last real effort to do the 12 steps? Do I think there might be some benefit for me today if I was to redo them?

3. In step two I was encouraged to work towards developing a belief in "a power greater than myself" which then might be able to do for me what I cannot do for myself. Steps three to nine created the opportunity for me to begin to develop and nurture a personal relationship with this Power. Did I ever really buy into this plan? If I did then, do I still feel the same way now?

4. Were steps ten to twelve ever really that important to me? Or did they simply become useful as foxhole exercises when a crisis appeared? If I did then, do I still feel the same way now? How important is living the spiritual life to me today? What has been my track record in this regard over recent months and maybe years?

5. On page 83 of our book it says "the spiritual life is not a theory, we have to live it." On page 51 "When many hundreds of people (the AA pioneers who wrote the book) are able to say that the consciousness of the Presence of God is today the most important fact of their lives, they present a powerful reason why one should live in faith." And finally on page 53 "When we became alcoholics, crushed by a self-imposed crisis we could not postpone or evade, we had to fearlessly face the proposition that God is everything or else He is nothing. God either is or He isn't. What was our choice to be?" Have I, or am I even willing to try accepting these statements as being literally true in my case? Can I see these statements as being at least equally as important to me today as they were in earlier recovery?

When we began our spiritual search we imagined that what we were seeking was information. Answers to questions like: Why am I an alcoholic? Why do I suffer so much? What must I do to free myself from this misery? Ultimately we discover there are no such answers to be found. There is only the simple reality of either living in addiction or living in sobriety and living in the grip of compulsive behavior or living in the absence of such behavior. Meaning is not found in what we read or hear, but in the reality of what we perceive when our personal lens through which we see the world become cleared of the fog of untreated alcoholism and/or addictions.

Of course, at the root of our addiction, as always, is that compulsive drive to control and manipulate life as it impacts us. By the way, this delusion to control and manipulate is not the sole domain of the alcoholic. Many experts in the fields of psychology and psychiatry suggest that it is an inherent disease equally common to all of humankind.

If we choose to believe that God's bounty is infinite and it is only ourselves who is the determiner and limiter of how much of His grace we will accept, then we can open our hearts and embrace the reality of truly limitless possibilities and act on it. Only then will we be able to experience those results that were previously just hopes and in some cases even unimaginable dreams. Ultimately, it is up to us, no one else can do it for us. Let us consider the following invitation. As only He can:
"BE NOT AFRAID: COME FOLLOW ME: AND I SHALL LEAD YOU HOME."

"At this point we do not submit, instead, we surrender. We do not recant, we become calm. We do not despise: We wonder *and ultimately become still and find acceptance without complaint, of all that is. We find ourselves marveling at the fact that someone like us is able to perceive this magnificent chaos that is the Great Reality. This is really God's will for our lives: To be still in the midst of all the madness and chaos that is humanity and to know that it is all God.*"

~ Rami Shapiro~

SOME THOUGHTS WORTH CONSIDERING

1. Prayer is not a "spare wheel" that you pull out when in trouble, but it is a "steering wheel" that directs the right path throughout.

2. So why is a car's windshield so large and the rear view mirror so small? It is because our past is not as important as our future. So, look ahead and move on.

3. The most powerful and life altering message I have ever received came to me as a two word, five letter statement….. "God is!"

4. Where love rules, there is no will for power; and where power predominates, there love is lacking. One is the shadow of the other.

5. When what we demand from life does not conform to what life has to offer and our kit of spiritual tools is nowhere to be found, we are in deep trouble.

6. The opinion which other people have of you is their problem, not yours. When you can accept this truth without question then you will be liberated from a self-created curse.

EINSTEIN: WHAT I BELIEVE!
(Albert Einstein's Creed)

In our search for spiritual growth it is essential to not only include the altruistic views of the spiritualists but also the pragmatic views of those humanists whose opinions are widely valued. Albert Einstein is without doubt one of such individuals.

Whether we know it or not, all human beings are in fact seeking the same thing. We may describe it differently but that is of no real consequence. For this alcoholic that inner need can best be described as the compelling spiritual need to simply return home. This spiritual home is not a physical place but rather an internal state of being.

A state of being is different from a state of mind. A state of being is much more inclusive than a state of mind. A state of being not only includes the intellect; it also incorporates one's emotions and feelings at a cognitive or conscious level. But a state of being, by necessity also includes that inner most part of ourselves wherein only our true identity can be found. That place where our soul, or if you prefer, our spirit resides.

A true state of conscious well-being is always transient and elusive but, when present for that moment, does provide us with that same special sense of security, peace and comfort that we all have experienced and cherished as children. For instance; who of us do not lovingly harbor some sort of childhood memory of returning home from some type of uncomfortable, insecure and possibly fearful life experience or excursion to once again embrace the safety, warmth, comfort and love of home?

As adults, the physical form of that childhood home and our parents or their surrogates are now gone but that natural craving for the same physical, psychological, emotional and spiritual comfort is even more compelling than it was when we were children. As spiritually broken adults we were without options so relied solely, wholly and only on alcohol and/or other chemicals to fill the void. Of course they eventually let us down and we became utterly helpless and hopeless in regards to our trying to cope with life. We were faced with two options. To either give up and wait for the end or to reach out for help are the only two choices. If you are reading this, you obviously are opting for the latter.

Let us make the most of this opportunity. You can be absolutely sure that the actions inherent in doing the twelve steps will, by necessity, most definitely result in a 180 degree shift from a negative to a positive personal state being for you personally. I believe Albert Einstein intuitively knew this and in his own way described it as follows.

In 1930, Albert Einstein composed a kind of creed he titled **"What I Believe,"** at the conclusion of which he wrote:

"To sense that behind everything that can be experienced there is something that our minds cannot grasp and whose beauty and sublimity reaches us only indirectly; this is religiousness. In this sense - I am devoutly a religious man."

In AA today we probably would understand what he meant by religion as being what we call spiritual.

In response to a young girl who had asked him whether or not he believed in God, Einstein wrote:

"Everyone who is seriously involved in the pursuit of science becomes convinced that there is a spirit manifested in the laws of the Universe – a spirit vastly superior to that of man." (I suspect that this was as close as Einstein would allow himself to come to refer to a Creator.)

And during a talk at Union Theological Seminary on the relationship of religion and science, Einstein declared:

"The situation may best be expressed by an image: Science without religion is lame, religion without science is blind."

We interpret this to mean that there is more needed to comprehend the Great Reality than simply intellect.

At this point we may do well to be reminded of the simple statement of true humility uttered by that "devil may care young chap" soon to be known as AA #4, shortly after being visited in the hospital by Bill, Doctor Bob and Bill D.

"Who am I to say there is no God?"

Can I now, at least for this moment, set aside my intellectual arrogance and become open to God's grace?

If you will allow me a personal note: Along with many nudges of encouragement from my sponsor, my new friends and of course the inspired text of our Big Book, I suspect strongly that in my own struggle in finding and experiencing faith the above statement was of significant influence in my coming face to face with the fallacy of my own inherent denial and prejudice towards a power greater than myself.

My recognition and eventual acceptance of AA number four's sudden "awakening" undoubtedly served as a stepping stone towards humility and a starting point towards the ultimate discovery of my own personal core belief. Today, I can share that core belief with you in the following which I now use as a mantra to help me refocus my thinking when I get emotionally caught up and distracted by the often frantic and chaotic events of daily living.

God Is! God is in me!
God is as me! God is me!
Wherever I go; He goes!
No beginning and no end!
Amen!

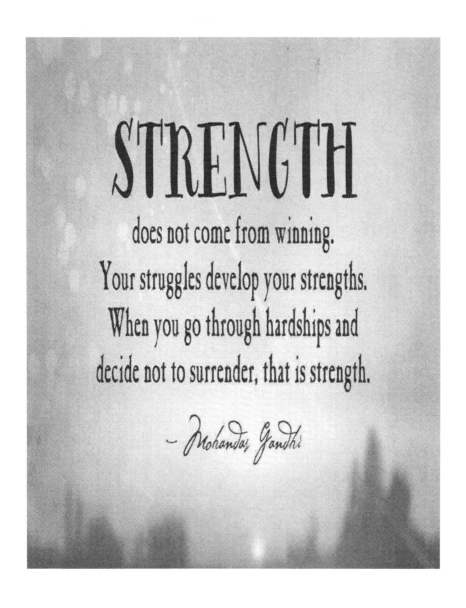

This chapter of our common journey comes to an end with the offer of the following gift just for you. We have gained access to what our Big Book calls "a kit of spiritual tools" for healthy living. For some of us alcoholics in recovery, the following poem/prayer is adapted from Max Erhmann's *Desiderata* and is considered by many in recovery to be a short list of at least some of those items in the kit.

DESIRED THINGS

Go calmly amid the noise and haste and remember what peace there may be in silence.

As far as possible, and without surrender be on good terms with all persons.

Speak your truth quietly and clearly and listen to others; their stories contain valuable lessons.

Avoid loud and aggressive persons; they add nothing positive to the spirit.

Comparing yourself to others is harmful and often self-demeaning because there will always be greater and lesser persons than yourself.

Stay interested in your own endeavors however humble they may be for they are your source of purpose and usefulness.

Most importantly, be honest with others by being yourself.

Nurture strength of spirit to shield you in sudden misfortune.

Beyond a wholesome self-discipline, be gentle with yourself for you are a child of the universe, no less than the trees and the stars; you have a right to be here.

And whether or not it is clear to you; no doubt the universe is unfolding as it should.

Be at peace with God. However you conceive Him to be.

Whatever your labors and aspirations in this noisy confusion of life, keep peace with your soul. It is still a beautiful world, strive to be happy.

STEP TWELVE

Having had a spiritual awakening as the result of these steps we tried to carry this message to other alcoholics and practice these principles in all of our affairs.

"No matter how unreasonable others may seem, I am responsible for not reacting negatively. Regardless of what is happening around me I will always have the prerogative, and the responsibility, of choosing what happens within me. I am the creator of my own reality. When I [review my day], I know that I must stop judging others. If I judge others, I am probably judging myself. Whoever is upsetting me most is my best teacher. I have much to learn from him or her, and in my heart, I should thank that person."

~ Bill W ~

COMMENTS ON LEARNING AND RECOVERY

Let us begin with a quote from Tom Brady, a long-time sober member of Alcoholics Anonymous (deceased).

"Real learning results in a permanent change of behavior, brought about by sustained practice of new information and ideas that we have acquired. Behavior includes how we respond to the people and events occurring around us, such as when we meet someone: Are we more interested in hearing what they have to say or is our primary interest more about telling them what is on our mind? More importantly, behavior also involves our habitual thinking, metaphorically such as; is the glass half empty or half full? More specifically, is our thinking mostly self- centred; or not? Is our thinking positive or negative?"

Working the 12 steps, attending AA meetings, reading the big book, including other AA recovery literature, is how we acquire information about alcoholism and possible recovery, including suggestions and example offered by and through more experienced sober members of AA.. This information is vital to help us deal with our disease and to live life effectively. To change behaviour, we first have to identify what it is about ourselves that is inappropriate (step 4 and 5) and then make a conscious effort to practice the newly learned behavior. This practice must occur over and over again until it becomes automatic (habit). This perseverance takes not only God's help (step 7) but also persistent mental commitment and effort on our part over an extended period of time.

In order to change our habitual thinking or mental behavior, we have to take sufficient time each day to meditate and pray in solitude (step 11). Not only must we ask that God help us to identify and have the courage to change our negative thinking but we must also exercise the personal discipline and commitment, on a continuing basis, to practice these new ways of positive thinking and to persevere until they become habit. A great deal of personal effort is required, but the ultimate rewards are priceless.

There is one particular aspect of our self-evaluation that we should be sceptical about. This is the question concerning how much time we should spend trying to love ourselves. Fortunately for us, we was told early on in our recovery to not waste one more second of time trying to learn to like ourself. Instead, we were directed only to focus our energies towards carrying out all of the suggested actions spelled out in the twelve steps to the very best of our abilities. We were told that if we would do only that, everything else including our self-image would be taken care of.

Since that time we have tried our best to follow that advice and in hind sight we are very grateful that we did. The truth is, that there is little more unlovable than an active untreated alcoholic, whether he is in his cups or not. We arrived at the doors of AA loathing our-selves. We had to learn that in our present condition, we could not possibly find our-self acceptable until we had actually done something to merit such approval. The twelve steps, obviously, provides a realistic set of positive actions to facilitate the acquiring of such essential approval.

This business of facilitating a fundamental change within our self is best stated in the truth: "W*e cannot think our way into right living but we can live way into right thinking*". Let us make our efforts positive, sustainable and worthwhile. Doing the next right thing are the daily marching orders for any recovering alcoholic and, is an essential skill learned only through continual trying and personal experience.

Recovery is a life-long process. The good news is that each day we are asked to simply do the best we can with what we have. Some days we can bring more to the table than we can on other days. As always, it is the effort that counts. Recovery is a process, not a destination. Although they appear to be impossible absolutes, the programs goals are really only provided to help keep us moving in the right direction.

Because life can only give back to you what you give to it, (The Law of Attraction) and because it is not reality itself that impacts us at a personal level, but it is really our *perception* of reality that is the real determiner, the following quote is of some considered significance.

> *One of the most important decisions you will ever make is the choosing of the kind of universe you exist in: Is it helpful and supportive or hostile and lonely? Your answer to this question will make all the difference in terms of how you live your life and ultimately what kind of Divine assistance you attract.*
>
> ~Wayne Dyer~

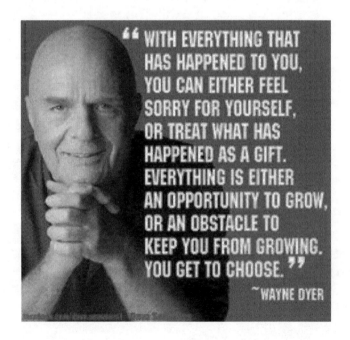

The following is an article written by a woman who, at the time, served as Spiritual Director for the Hazelden/Betty Ford Treatment Center. Because this particular message speaks so directly to the same "keys" of recovery as does this workbook, she has kindly agreed to allow us to include it here.

LIVING THE TWELVE STEPS
~JoAnn C.-R.~

We recently moved, and I'm now shopping for a step ladder so I can reach my cupboards. Because it will be a permanent fixture in the kitchen, this ladder must be durable, sturdy, tall and elegant. It's not a big leap to see that the Twelve Steps also function this way in my life—they lift me to a better place and allow me to reach what I want, if I just use them.

I can only live the Twelve Steps if, at some point, I've taken the actions they require under the guidance of a sponsor. It's not enough to go to meetings and talk about them, or hear how others have worked the Steps. I have to follow the principles myself, with help and support, to become spiritually fit. Spiritual fitness, which is the buffer zone between what happens in the world and how I respond to it, is much like physical fitness.

I don't get lean by drinking coffee and talking about treadmills. I actually have to walk. Taking the actions for each Step as outlined in Alcoholics Anonymous (AA) allows two things to occur, simultaneously.

The first thing is that my ego is deflated and my

personality is changed; my inner addict goes into the back seat by taking actions that level my pride, confess my shortcomings, and require self-searching (AA p. 25).

The second thing that working the Steps does is nourish my "innermost self" (AA p. 30, my spirit—the healthy me, always connected to a Higher Power—by ensuring that I make an honest, authentic connection with myself, others or a Higher Power in each Step. I receive benefits, results, and promises when I take these actions.
Once I've worked the Steps I have new skills to cope with life when things get hard, skills I have to practice daily to live happily in recovery. Perhaps the one line that best sums up the perspective I gain by working the Twelve Steps is the following:

"It is a spiritual axiom that every time we are disturbed, no matter what the cause, there is something wrong with us"

This line in the Step Ten essay in the Twelve Steps and Twelve Traditions shows me when I need to double up on my spiritual activities—anytime I'm disturbed. Living in the solution of these steps, I can no longer point fingers or blame others for my emotional imbalance. Whenever I'm disturbed, I must search within myself for the cause. That's the essence of conducting a daily inventory. I can't afford to let irritability and restlessness become my norm.

When I was active in my addictions, I thought my happiness depended on things external to me changing. I needed the perfect mate, the right body size, a certain number in the bank account, and other people to always behave with kindness and understanding. Since that wasn't possible, I drank or got high in order to escape a reality that wasn't pleasing to me.

In recovery, I am responsible for my own happiness. So today when I'm off center, I have a set of tools to inventory what's going on in me, identify what I need to do to come back into balance, and, if I find myself not using the tool, I can call on others who understand these principles and pray to a higher power to help me use them promptly and properly.

What does it look like to live the Twelve Steps? I've taken the essence of each step and put it into a suggestion for lifelong recovery.

1. Embrace the presence of the Holy (guides, angels, teachers, higher power, God) as the path to a better life.

2. Be wide open to life, no expectations or fears, no preconceived ideas or concerns.

3. Be willing to be changed. Knowing and not knowing are both acceptable states of being.

4. Be totally honest in my questions, hurts, desires, dreams and longings. That level of honesty with self makes me less tempted to control others.
5. Hold nothing back from a sponsor or a home group. Share it all, not just what I think they want to hear.

6. Love myself—the good and the bad. Laugh at mistakes and give up on perfection. We can't do this wrong and stretching is how we all grow.

7. Seek help when things get hard. Stop worrying about past mistakes. People were hurt because that's how they interpreted things. I was hurt because of my story and interpretation. Shift internally and act differently.

8. Love the people in front of me—strangers in cars, the lover in the bed, the sister on the phone, the friend obsessed with his pain. Love them all and watch wounds heal.

9. Be totally present. This is the only moment, so hold it gently and savor it.

10. Open to the divine often. It is always available, accessible and even eager.
11. Do not pray for answers only, but for affirmation, assurance, and enjoy the sheer pleasure of that connection.

12. Be helpful. Share what I know now without waiting for it to be perfect. Say Yes to life's invitations whether I think I'm ready or not.

The best part of living the Twelve Steps is I don't do it alone—I have a community who interprets the world through a similar lens, a sponsor who freely shares how she's navigated challenges, and an increasingly close relationship with the holiest part of myself, the world, and others that shows me time and again that this world is a marvelous place, that nothing really goes wrong, and that there's always a new opportunity to do it better today. Today, I'm happy with what is and eager for more. This is the path to growth and fulfillment I've been seeking my entire life.

When having trouble with acceptance you may wish to consider the following.

My mind is at peace knowing that what is meant for me will never miss me, and that which misses me was never meant for me.

~Buddha~

Concerning the thoughts we allow to linger in our consciousness: Negative thoughts act like a cancer to the spirit. They need to be identified and excised as soon as possible. We do this through The Step 7 Prayer along with conscious effort on our part to direct our thinking and actions towards others and what we might do to add to their wellbeing.

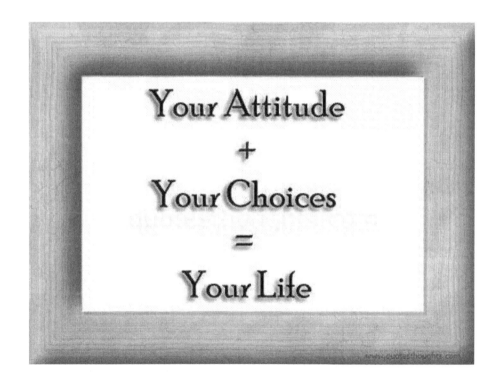

A MEMBERS EYE VIEW OF ALCOHOLICS ANONYMOUS

*The following is borrowed from an AA pamphlet titled *'A Members Eye View of Alcoholics Anonymous'*. The portion reprinted below is from the end of a transcript of a talk the author made to a group of addictions counselling students many years ago. This message he carried to them then is just as real and powerful today as it was the day it was first delivered.

"Ladies and gentlemen, who would dare to attempt to analyze a phenomenon, or diagram a wonder, or parse a miracle? The answer is: Only a fool. And I trust that tonight, I have not been such a fool. All I have tried to tell you is where I have been these last 16 years and some of the things I have come to believe because of my journeying.

This coming Sunday in the churches of many of us, there will be read that portion of the Gospel of Matthew which recounts the time when John the Baptist was languishing in the prison of Herod and hearing of the works of his cousin Jesus, he sent two of his disciples to say to him, "Art thou he who is to come, or shall we look for another?"

And Christ did as he so often did. He did not answer them directly. But wanting John to decide for himself he said to the disciples: Go and report to John only what you have heard and only what you have seen: Tell John that the blind see: The lame walk: The lepers are cleansed: The deaf hear: The dead rise" And the poor have the gospel preached to them.

Back in my childhood catechism days, I was taught that the word "poor" in this instance did not only mean to be poor in a material sense, but also to be "poor in spirit"; those who burned with an inner thirst and an inner hunger to satiate their very real and painful emptiness: And that the word "gospel" quite literally means "the good news."

More than 16 years ago, four men – my boss, my physician, my pastor and the one friend I had left – working singly and together, maneuvered me into AA. Tonight, if they were to ask me, "Tell us: What did you find?" I would say to them what I now say to you.

I can tell you only what I have seen and only what I have heard: And it seems to me that the blind do see: The lame do walk: The lepers are indeed cleansed: The deaf do hear: And the dead do rise. And over and over again through the middle of the longest day and into the darkest night: The poor in spirit alcoholics have the good news of our program brought to them. May God grant that this will always be so."

Our journey through the 12 steps is just about over. In recovery as in all life's experiences, each ending leads immediately to a new beginning.

When we started this particular adventure, we were promised that if we were diligent in applying ourselves to this exercise, we would discover, at some point down the road, that we have in fact changed and the changes are clearly for the better. And when we become touched by these moments of revelation we can only express our gratitude by humbly saying thank you to our Higher Power working for us through the miracle of the twelve steps.

What follows is a reminder yet again that it is our thinking and perceptions that is the direct determiner of our reality and obviously, our state of mind. When we arrived at the doors of Alcoholics Anonymous we were the helpless victims of an undisciplined mind that ultimately made it impossible to experience little more than diseased thinking and discomfort. Today, with God's help, it becomes possible to learn to live a sane, purposeful, positive, fulfilling and rewarding life.

> *The soul is dyed the color of its thoughts. Think only on those things in line with your principles and you can bear the light of day. The content of your character is your choice. Day by day, what you choose, what you think and what you do is who you become. Your integrity through your thoughts and actions is your destiny ... it is the light that guides your way.*
> ~ Hercules ~

"I am fundamentally an optimist. Whether that comes from nature or nurture, I cannot say. Part of being optimistic is keeping one's head pointed toward the sun, one's feet moving forward. There were many dark moments when my faith in humanity was sorely tested, but I would not and could not give myself up to despair. That way lays defeat and death."

~ Nelson Mandela ~

LIVING WITH STEP ONE IN RECOVERY

As motivated recovering alcoholics we become committed to putting the 12 steps into practice in our daily lives. By now we have learned that recovery begins as an intellectual exercise (learning new ideas and practices) but ultimately must become an experiential exercise (putting the new way of life into practice). With diligence, along with the passage of time, we will without a doubt, reach a point whereby staying away from the next drink becomes a noticeably less acute problem; if a problem at all. It becomes evident that we are able to surrender the drink problem for prolonged periods of time easily into the hands of the Higher Power of our own understanding such that we usually have no thought whatsoever of wanting a drink.

On those occasions when the thought of drinking does arise, there is now little or no discomfort associated with that thought and it quickly disappears. It becomes quite evident that if there is anything at all in our recovery program that can be done 100%, it is this surrendering of the drink problem on a daily basis. This is the greatest possible blessings we alcoholics could ever hope for. Each day we face requires us to put into play those actions that provide us with this priceless gift.

Of course, this is not news to any alcoholic who has walked the walk of recovery for any significant period of time. However: With respect to the second part of step one, "... our lives had become unmanageable," we may not be so effectively accommodated.

Speaking from experience, we can tell you that as time passes, and "not drinking" transitions from being a difficult challenge to becoming something of a novelty and eventually to a state of normalcy, we are in greater and greater danger of taking our recovery for granted. If or when this happens we are more likely to not continue doing our due diligence with respect to the second part of step one.

Let there be no misunderstanding: Putting the drink issue aside, at some point in our recovery, we will come to understand and accept the following truth.

Our unmanageable life was not caused by our drinking.
Our unmanageable life was THE cause of our drinking.

We know this to be true because during our drinking days our countless failed attempts to manage and manipulate life's outcomes to suit our own personal desires was the prime cause of our being "restless, irritable and discontented," which was a seemingly persistent state of mind for most of us. The resulting discomfort always left us with no choice but to eventually succumb once again to the insidious demand to have a few drinks in order to take the pressure off. We did this repeatedly even though we knew full well of all the havoc, chaos and pain that would inevitably follow. We were without choice.

Later, in step 4, we became aware of the fact that our only real problem and the one problem which will require active, daily, and often moment to moment attention for the rest of our life is our self-centred insistence to want to continue to "run our own show" even though, in our heart, we know it is futile and self-destructive. We believe that this need to control life emanates from our ego and its innate fear of losing control of personal security and self-esteem. This futile and self-deceptive attempt to soothe those fears is today, even more subtle and problematic than it was when we were drinking. We never seem to lose the need to try to continue to deceive ourselves. With persistence we can however look forward to measurably lessening the problem.

Our real living problem today and that which will continue to be our challenge for every day of the rest of our life will be to recognize when we are suffering symptoms of this unrequited and insane self-centred demand that life provide us with what we want instead of what we need and then once more, surrender ourselves to the hopelessness of our folly and immediately turn our will and our life over to the care of God as we understand Him. Ultimately, this is the only way to find honest relief. We must always exercise humility and recognize our powerlessness by honestly and humbly accepting life as it comes and we can do this now because we surrender our self-will to God so that we may be returned to effective and positive living.

Despite appearances, we need to always remember that the universe is in fact unfolding exactly as it is supposed to and therefore all is well. Only when we know this in our heart can peace of mind return.

By the way, as a side bar; and for your interest only, this need to control people and circumstances around us is so universal that many of the professionals tell us that: "The need to control" is the most common mental addiction (obsession) found throughout all of mankind.

How this problem may affect the non-alcoholics is for us a moot point. However for we who are alcoholic, if left unchecked, this mental obsession to control is deadly. If allowed free reign, it will once again make life so miserable for us that we will inevitable return to drink and experience all of the now predictable consequences that result and the downward physical, mental and spiritual spiral will pick up right where it left off when we began our recovery and in short order, life will once again be too painful to bear and we once again become trapped in that intolerable and hopeless state of mind and body.

May God grant that we never lose the humility to recognize that we are powerless not only over alcohol but over the totality of life itself. Only then will we turn to God in all of our affairs! Only then will we know the true meaning of the words "of myself I am nothing, it is the Father that doeth the works"! Only then will we will we know the true meaning of the three most important words in all of twelve step recovery;

ACCEPT - SURRENDER - TRUST!

*Just to be clear. When we who write this missive use the term "to know God," we certainly do not suggest that one might understand God. We simply mean to experience through our feelings and emotions the presence of God within us. To know God is totally an experiential phenomenon and therefore different from a belief in God which is totally cognitive and centred in the brain.

SIMPLY FOR YOUR CONSIDERATION

Carefully watch your thoughts, for they become your words.
Manage and watch your words, for they will become your actions.
Consider and judge your actions, for they will become your habits.
Acknowledge and watch your habits, for they will become your values.
Understand and embrace your values, for they will become your destiny. (Gandhi)

"A star falls from the sky and into your hands. Then it seeps through your veins and swims inside your blood and becomes every part of you. And then you have to put it back into the sky. And it's the most painful thing you'll ever have to do and that you've ever done. But what's yours is yours; whether it's up in the sky or here in your hands. And one day, it'll fall from the sky and hit you in the head real hard and that time, you won't have to put it back in the sky again." (Joy Bell

"Is sobriety all that we are to expect of a spiritual awakening? Most definitely NO, sobriety is only the bare beginning; it is only the first gift of the first awakening. If more gifts are to be received, our awakening has to go on. As it does go on, we find that bit by bit we can discard the old life - the one that did not work - for a new life that can and does work under any conditions whatever." (Bill W)

The next essay will be a look at what we have come to appreciate to be the most challenging and difficult part of our spiritual journey to date. It is an effort that we have come to believe takes us to what we suspect may be the very limits of what any human being might be capable of reaching.

What we are going to talk about is something that Bill Wilson first wrote about in the 1958 Grapevine titled *The Next Frontier: Emotional Sobriety.*

Because the human condition by definition confines us to a world view/reality bounded by time and space, we are forever limited in our ability to directly perceive anything that does not conform to being physical and measurable. Our search for our own spirituality asks us to go beyond the physical world and asks that we consider such metaphysical possibilities as infinity, timelessness and more importantly the possible reality of a universal and unifying spirit.

We know for certain that human life has a definite beginning and end. But we also know that the elusive but essential part of our human makeup commonly referred to as the human spirit evidently was pre-existing and came to us from somewhere else and: After our physical death, will continue to exist ad infinitum. The question we are investigating here is whether or not there might be some way we can facilitate a personal connection between our finite human (physical) self and our infinite, spiritual self. For your consideration, we offer you our humble and woefully inadequate efforts in this regard, to date.

BECOMING A SPIRITUAL SEEKER
(A Journey beyond the 12 Steps)

What comes next may or may not be of interest to you. First, a friendly warning: Please be mindful that if ventured into, what follows is a totally personal and private journey and may force you to expand your comfort zone. What we are talking about is a process of nurturing and growing our spiritual life and will include, by necessity, our personal relationship with the world around us.

That being said: If you are like us, and may be interested in trying to improve the quality and meaning of your life, and also believe that further growth will demand effort on your part, then what follows might well be of interest to you.

Psychologists tell us that as untreated alcoholics, we are both cognitively and emotionally immature. We come to learn in recovery that it is equally true that sooner or later we must come to know this and address this deficiency if we are to ever find long term sobriety. This psychological immaturity we displayed had nothing to do with our age or the legal definition of being an adult. It is a state of mind. In fact, this psychological immaturity is the first and most necessary state of mind of all young and inexperienced children. It is what the spiritual seeker/mystic Richard Rohr (among others) calls *"dualistic thinking."* More will be said about this later.

Many of us in recovery today, and totally through the eyes of hindsight, willingly confess that we only became willing and ultimately able to grow up and become more responsible adults totally as the direct consequence of applying the principles of good living learned from the practice of implementing the 12 steps in our daily affairs.

We have come to believe that this necessary transition from psychological and emotional immaturity to a more responsible adulthood may simply mean the paradigm shift of one's focus from being completely inward looking and exclusive, to growing more outward looking and inclusive in regards to our relationship to the world and its people around us. In the Big Book, this is what Silkworth was talking about as being *"the essential psychic change" necessary* for an alcoholic to recover through personal application of the twelve steps. This is where spiritual growth can help us.

Let us be perfectly clear. We the writers have come to believe the following to be true: Reality, or if you prefer, "all that is"; can never be in dispute, at least among the sane and rational. Also, this stuff called reality is, of itself without assessment. Neither is it good nor bad, right or wrong, positive or negative. All of that is simply the product of an individual making a personal judgement or evaluation.

It is at this point that differences in thinking between individuals, will inevitably crop up. This is because, for reasons discussed later, we all evaluate our circumstances (reality) subjectively and come to personal conclusions, sometimes called opinions, or maybe beliefs and in extreme cases, personal truths. These differences only become socially damaging and corrupting when we mistakenly think that our personal truths are in fact reality when it really is no such thing. The simple truth is, *reality is what it is; it is the interpretation of reality that is the difference maker.*

We constantly evaluate our ever changing surroundings and circumstances in order to determine how the reality of the moment affects our personal security and wellbeing. This process of evaluation is instinctive. It is an essential part of the human tool kit for survival. Because all of us have acquired our own unique set of life and learning experiences, there are filters through which we interpret the world and are all uniquely different one from another. The result therefore always results in different opinions, points of view, biases and prejudices which are the fodder for potential arguments, intolerance and even hatred. Just look at social media today, public radicalization and especially inter party political dialogue. Too much of it is unfortunately divisive, often vile and contemptable.

We must learn to accept the fact that we can never escape our own embedded biases and prejudices completely for the simple reason that mentally we can never totally disconnect ourselves from ourselves. The statement **"wherever I go: I go!"** is undeniably and absolutely true. That being said, what follows can be helpful in leading us to a somewhat more open minded perspective and with that, hopefully a reduction of conflict within and between ourselves and others. Only then can we build towards greater acceptance, tolerance and open mindedness. Knowing this to be so may be essential in finding true wisdom and is the first giant step we can personally make towards finding what Rohr calls the second and most meaningful stage of life. We will discuss this second stage of life shortly.

But first, as children and in honest simplicity, we see ourselves at the centre of the universe as we know it and have full expectations, if not demands, that all that we need and want should be provided for us and that of ourselves, we are without fault. Whenever something does go wrong or does not happen the way we think it should, it is always the fault of someone or something else; never is it us. We always see ourselves as innocent victims in these circumstances.

This is the first stage of life; a kind of dualistic world, wherein we see ourselves as a unique identity separate and distanced from the rest of the universe. As the result, our reality is totally defined by how successful we are at being able to get our needs fulfilled with or without the cooperation of others. Because of our perceived separateness we form alliances with others having similar interests (needs) and stand prepared to compete with opposing interests. Cooperation is always dependent on self-interests being addressed first with the common interests always a secondary consideration.

As blossoming adults, by necessity, we will have to acquire a much different and less self-centred perception of the world if we want to have any hope of finding any real wellbeing. Only then are we able to see that in fact, we are not the centre of the real world at all. We are definitely significant and of real value but, we are in truth, just one small piece of something much greater than ourselves. At this point, the new idea of "fitting in", cooperation and accommodation hopefully become operative.

We inevitably must come to know the truth that this greater reality of which we are a part is governed by irrefutable laws of harmony and order and if we are going to be able to function at all effectively and purposefully in this true reality we must humbly accept and embrace our own responsibility to operate symbiotically within the boundaries defined by these higher moral and ethical truths. Our well-being will ultimately be determined by precisely the degree to which we turn away from self-centred motives and interests towards those of connection, cooperation and unity with the greater world.

Next, as true adults we must know that legally and morally we have to be responsible for our own actions and in order to feel worthwhile, we must contribute in some meaningful way to the welfare of the community of which we are part. For many of us alcoholics, the psychological transition from limiting immaturity to adult maturity does not take place naturally or easily as it might in the so called normal, non-addicted individual but ultimately, it was only made possible later in recovery through our necessary surrender to the principles of the 12 steps. We hopefully discover in hindsight that the 12 steps were and are a necessary pathway for us to healthy daily living.

Psychologists also tell us that the other change that takes place in the transition from the child into the adult has to do with the recognition of our need to meaningfully pursue the fulfillment of the three basic needs common to all human beings that must be fulfilled in order for us to experience real wellbeing.

These three needs, in no particular order, can be stated as: First, finding a healthy persona (identity), second, finding *physical, emotional and psychological security*, and third, finding a meaningful sense of *usefulness or purpose*. As far as the alcoholic is concerned, the recognition of these needs is also delayed until the 12 steps of recovery become operative in our lives. However, when these changes do become operative in our life, this will, more than anything else, be what will enhance the nature and quality of any individual's sober life.

Every one of our journeys into recovery is, without doubt, a totally personal experience and for that reason is unique and different, for each and every one of us. This is true at least with regards to our perceptions and interpretations of our experiences. Similar experiences are very often perceived very differently, at least in part, due to the fact that we all have a uniquely different set of cognitive filters through which we view life and form our judgements, make assumptions and draw conclusions. Because of this fact, we will always have somewhat different interpretations of otherwise common experiences. However, there will always be universal and absolute agreement on the unifying and wholesome nature of the recovery process. Again, recovery is experiential (feelings); not intellectual (cognitive). The intellect is essential in getting us to recovery but is of itself not directly involved in recovery. Recovery is totally a spiritual (experiential) process. In simple terms, that means to surrender to the unknowable and to experience (feel to the core of your being) the peace and contentment that inevitably follows.

The fact is, many who have travelled this way before us and shared one with another, believe that our spiritual journeys and the cognitive and emotional experiences (growth) encountered along the way are far more similar, one to another, than they are different. Because understanding God is beyond comprehension by mere mortals, the only real, useful and unifying comparison to be made between individual experiences and journeys in this regard is with respect to what actually happens and not the explanations as to the how and why it happens. The how and the why questions are undoubtedly unanswerable and may be intellectually interesting but are really irrelevant to the experience of recovery itself.

Recovery will manifest itself whenever we are conscious of being connected (at one with) or in unity with, the world around us rather than the more usual and common condition of feeling separate or apart from. A condition sometimes described as being a witness to life rather than being a part of life. Some of the more religious among us describe this connection as *"being at one with God."* The simplest definition of recovery we can think of is the coming to know that we are no longer on the outside of life looking in, instead, we are on the inside of life now and are an active participant.

At those priceless moments of experiencing conscious unity with all that is, our basic needs of personal *identity, purpose and security* are overflowing in abundance. We intuitively enjoy a sense of fulfillment and completeness that can only be described as "out of this world" and for which we will instinctively crave for more. For many of us, we become conscious of experiencing true contentment and fulfillment.

On a personal note and once again through listening to and reading about the spiritual journeys from others who we the writers believe know far more than us, are lead to conclude that as imperfect beings, there is an undefinable and yet very real longing or craving emanating from very core of each and every one of us. This inner craving or need can be left unrequited and ignored in some of us for a very, very long time. As long as we allow this craving to remain unaddressed, we will continue to experience great unrest and consequently only limited happiness at best. More often than not, we experience conflict and chaos in our conscious reality. We probably did not know this when we entered recovery. Thankfully, today we know that addressing this spiritual need is what the 12 steps are all about. Most simply, this universal need can be best described as the need to know who we really are.

This same spiritual obsession can also be described as an "unrequited longing". We believe that this need crosses all genders, races, religions, age, education, politics or any other man made line of differentiation drawn between human beings. Because we recognize that our common genesis is *"The Universal Creator"* (however we may define it), our need or craving is to return home and be "as one" with this eternal spirit. Specifically, that means to be in the conscious presence of this *"One Universal Source"*. Once again, how we perceive this Universal Source is of no real consequence; it is only the experience of being in unity with it that matters.

Our real question at this point must be, how do we allow ourselves to experience the conscious presence of our creator and by so doing satisfy our spiritual hunger?

The only way we know how to do this is to practice what is called *contemplative prayer and meditation*. This means we will need to take the time to meditate by being still and being at peace both physically and mentally. To know, that at this moment of solitude, we are not separate from, but in fact at one with the universe and most importantly, at one with our *Universal Creator*.

By consciously taking the time to meditate repeatedly, we gain confidence, find confirmation, and spiritual strength by living in this very moment of time called the present moment. For it is at this very moment we cease to believe in the presence of God and delightfully we begin to **know the presence of God.**

When we take the time each day to be contemplative and to meditate in this manner we are then armed and ready to proceed with our day without fear or worry, trying only to do the next right thing as events and circumstances that we might otherwise be fearful unfold before us.

At this point, more needs to be shared about the nature and types of prayer available to us. Prayer takes many forms and it is important that we avail ourselves of the entire spectrum of prayer if we realistically are to expect positive results.

We suggest that prayer may be practiced in any one of four ways, based on where we are in our own spiritual life at any moment in time. We say this because our spiritual life like any other behavior or practice is never static. It is always fluid and always changing. Some days we are stronger, others we are less so.

The first and most basic stage of prayer is what we chose to call **recited prayer**. This form of prayer may be either spoken or silent: It may be practiced publicly or in private. This form of prayer involves our most basic cognitive function of basic recitation of written prayer either directly or by memory.

The second level of prayer is **reflective prayer** for which we focus our attention on the wording of some particular prayer or piece of scripture and consider what the significance of this specific message might mean to us at a personal level. At this point we are using our powers of cognition and judgement. This practice can be done privately or with others, as was the case with recited prayer. Once again we are dealing strictly at the cognitive level but adding the function of critical thinking such as evaluation or prioritization, along with the previously mentioned memory.

The third level of prayer can only be done alone and is not as well defined as the first two. This form of prayer is most commonly called **meditation.** Here we take time to reflect and consider, in a more general way, things like a self-evaluation (inventory taking), our relationship with our Higher Power, and most importantly an honest and critical look at our relationship with the people, events and circumstances we encounter in our daily life. Meditation can only occur when some significant level of mental quietness or calmness is operative, which of course applies to all prayer. Suggestions for creating conditions of calmness or quiet will be presented later. Meditation is a form of prayer that like the previous two is once again totally a cognitive practice, but now includes the most complex form of thinking which is called abstract thought. Abstract thought involves considering things that are not at the moment present and therefore cannot be evaluated or examined through our five basic senses.

The fourth and highest level of prayer has many names but for our purpose, we will refer to it as **contemplative prayer.** This is the most challenging form of prayer but also offers by far and away the greatest personal rewards. The true consequences of practicing contemplative prayer are what we believe to be what all alcoholics, addicts and in fact any human being who have ever been plagued by persistent feelings of inadequacy, incompleteness, failure or persistent anxiety and doubt have unknowingly and frustratingly been looking for throughout the life of their disease.

Most certainly, today we know that the payout from practicing contemplative prayer is what we alcoholics had been looking for through the bottom of every alcoholic drink we ever consumed. The payoff from contemplative prayer can lead a practitioner from simply having a belief in a Higher Power to actually knowing that Higher Power at a totally personal, and experiential level. *One's faith can be confirmed through contemplative prayer.* To learn how to practice contemplative prayer and dwell on the present moment without thinking, will not come naturally or easily. Most likely, none of us will ever become very good at it. However it is well worth the effort to keep trying because the payout does not depend so much on our skill or efficiency but much more so on our persistence and commitment to keep trying. This is the part of recovery we were told we will never complete and that it is the journey (practice) that is truly important, not the destination. The fact is the destination of our spiritual journey is not to be found in this life anyway. Our spiritual home exists beyond the confines of time and space that define this humanity based and always temporary universe as we understand it.

Let's next have a look at the real significance of what we call the present moment. It is the case that when we are actively thinking, which is what we are doing virtually continuously while awake, our brain can only deal with two parts of the triad of the human reality; (past, present, future): Namely our past and our future.
The present moment, in all reality, does not exist. It is true that the present can be artificially defined as a specific time period currently transpiring, such as the 24 hours making up today, but what about the real time existence of the so-called *present moment*? Can we actually capture that?

The truth is the present moment is totally beyond our cognitive power to dwell on because the so-called present moment is truly timeless. The present moment is no more than an identifier for that timeless and seamless bridge that connects our future with our past. It is only the past and the future that can be defined in terms of a specific time frame.

Most importantly, this very special but timeless moment called the present moment in the human experience is also our connection or bridge between the human universe defined by time and space and a second and parallel universe we will call the infinite universe. This infinite or spiritual universe is of course the *Domain of God the Father* and is the creative source from which our own eternal spirit has its genesis and to which, in time, it must leave this temporary human universe and return to its true home.

Mystics and simple seekers like us believe that Contemplative prayer represents the only human access point from our time and space universe to this parallel universe which is the true source of all that is and is in fact timeless. This is the home of our infinite Father and creator and also the true home of our personal spirit as well. Our spiritual need is to be at one with this natural home. This is the goal of contemplative.

To learn how to practice contemplative prayer and dwell on the present moment without thinking, will not come naturally or easily. Most likely, none of us will ever become very good at it. However it is well worth the effort to keep trying because the payout does not depend so much on our skill or efficiency but more so on our persistence and commitment to keep trying. This is the part of recovery we were told we will never complete and that it is the journey (practice) that is truly important, not the destination. The fact is the destination of our spiritual journey is not to be found in this life anyway. Our spiritual home exists beyond the confines of time and space that defines the limits of this humanity based universe as we understand it.

It is important to understand that we cannot learn to dwell on the present moment but we can learn to dwell **in** the present moment. In this case, the difference between

on and in means to be at one with the present moment, not separate from the present moment. It is absolutely impossible to dwell on the present. That manmade tool called time immediately pushes the thought/reality of the present moment into our past. In all honesty, when we are residing in the present moment we are without thought, but thoughtless in a good way.

The nature of contemplative prayer is to not think at all. Rather, we are trying to be totally focused on the reality of the present moment. It is suggested that when we do this we are in fact connected totally to the universe as it is and even more importantly connected directly to "The Creator" of all that is and obviously that must include ourselves. When we do this we have taken ourselves beyond the *thought* of being in the presence of God to actually **being in the presence of God.** This is an experiential moment not a cognitive moment. It cannot be explained, it can only be experienced. As stated earlier, this is the experience that feeds our soul and grows our faith. This is the way we properly satiate our three basic needs for personal security, purposefulness and identity; in other words to truly know who we really are. That disease driven spiritual thirst and hunger is finally satisfied.

As human beings, any intellectual concept of God by itself is hopelessly incomplete and inadequate: However, a more fulfilling and real spiritual experience may be generated through the practice of contemplative prayer. What we mean is that our relationship with God must be lived and not just thought about.

Our intellect controls the domain of dualistic thinking which is required to navigate the conscious universe defined by time and space. That piece of the human makeup commonly called the human spirit is what connects the otherwise earthly and finite human being with the infinite and eternal world of creation. Our conscious connection with our spirit appears to occur through our feelings and emotions. A spiritual experience can never properly be described, it only be lived. But it is only through such an experience that true peace of mind, wellness and completeness can be found.

Many of us who have "bought into" the exercise or practice described in the following prefer to call ourselves spiritual seekers, or more simply *"seekers"*. We prefer this label to that of the more traditional terms of mystical thinker or mystic. It is from the ancient mystics that the practice of contemplative prayer has its origins. We find simply being a seeker is far less pretentious and much more appropriate for we who have found our way to this point through humiliation. In fact, we arrived at this point not by design but rather by accident, as the result of self-inflicted failure and great pain. The true mystics found their way to contemplative prayer motivated not by humiliation and pain but rather through true humility and great love to know God that created not only themselves but in fact all that is. Yes! There are many true mystics alive today. You will know them when you see them. Listen carefully to what they tell you. Their message is important.

If what you read so far is attractive to you, I suggest that you give the following suggestions a try. Be warned: To be contemplative does not come easy because learning to "not think" is contrary to the ingrained habits of our brain. Failure will likely precede success in this venture. This is truly a case where practice is the objective, certainly not perfection.

To begin to practice contemplative prayer you will need to set aside time on a daily basis for a period of solitude. It is suggested that we should devote at least twenty minutes at the start of the day and a similar twenty minutes before retiring at night to do the following.

First, we must clear our mind of the chaotic and confusing thoughts resulting from the noise and clamour of daily living. The objective of the exercise is to clear the mind in order to achieve as close to a thoughtless and totally receptive state of mind as possible or at the very least, a mind that is quiet and hopefully calm. Often, this will take considerable time. Please persevere. This process can be helped in a number of ways. One may begin by focusing our eyes and attention totally on one particular simple object in our line of sight. That could be as simple as a leaf on a tree nearby or for that matter, anything else in our surroundings. Any non-moving object will suffice. As well, any constant repetitive auditory or tactile stimuli are equally useful.

We then focus our attention solely on that one constant environmental stimulus, blocking out all else. We try not to think. It is the constancy of the stimuli we focus on that is important. Not thinking is the key. *We want to experience dwelling only in the moment.*

By doing this we are attempting to experience being directly connected to the infinite and eternal universe of which we are a part. We are trying to become connected with or if you prefer, *at one with* all that is. This is what we believe is the spirit's natural state of being. We are trying to create a conscious awareness of personal wholeness incorporating and uniting all of our mind, body and spirit into total oneness.

Our ego, by its very nature, demands that we identify ourselves as being separate and distinct from the rest of the universe. However, the perception of being separated or alone is spiritually an unnatural state. To overcome this often fear-full and otherwise uncomfortable condition, we must get our ego and the self focused thoughts resulting out of way, if only for brief moments. This will require disciplined repetitive mental effort. Because we cannot stop thinking totally, we can also help ourselves in this mental decluttering process by thinking of some meaningful but simple repetitive prayer or saying.

To be sure; to know God and to understand God are two entirely different things. No one in his right mind would dare to suggest having an understanding of the omniscient. *When we say "to know God" we mean to simply and consciously experience the presence of God's "Holy Spirit" within us.* We believe that God, who expresses himself in us as "The Holy Spirit", and our own spirit are in fact one and the same and therefore absolutely inseparable.

Our human challenge always has been and always will be to separate our self-centered thinking which is very limited and can only relate to a world of individuals and separateness, (me being over here and you being over there) from the true and real world of oneness and unity, created in perfect unity by the Holy Spirit constantly flowing in, through and around us all.

Only in perfect solitude can we experience God's presence and hear His voice. One such affirmation that was recommended to us is the following prayer adapted from psalm 46, verse 10.

BE STILL

Be still and know that I am God
Be still and know that I love you.
Be still and know that I am your rock
And your shield
Be still and know that I am in you,
I am as you and I am you.
Be still and know that wherever
You go I also go.
Be still and know that we are one
And together forever.
Amen.

~Anonymous~

For most of us, our sense of self and all the limitations inherent in it has become both the dominant and also our default way of thinking. Self centred thinking, when left unchecked, will quickly release all of the so-called "children of the ego" thoughts (those addressed in steps 6 and 7) into our conscious reality and keep us in a seemingly constant state of restlessness, irritability and discontent. Contemplative prayer provides a respite from our lesser self and a way out.

One last suggestion: It is found in the historic records from Judaism's earliest days that the ancient followers were avid practitioners of contemplative prayer and for the sake of humility they were not allowed to refer to God, the unknowable, by name. Over the centuries, these contemplatives came up with a number of different terms to be used in referencing God. The one term that has withstood the test of time and continues to be the most oft reference to God is the word *"Yahweh"*.

It is said that this word *"Yahweh"*, when pronounced correctly, is the only known word that can be said without moving one's lips or tongue and is, when pronounced properly, the precise sound created when one inhales and then exhales. Yahweh is the sound of breathing; Yahweh is the sound of life itself.

To focus on ones breathing is an excellent method to help eliminate the extraneous clutter from the mind and create that peace and calmness essential to experience the contemplative state. This practice can also help us to truly experience and enjoy the moment of perfect unity and love with our Creator and "be at peace".

At this point, we leave you with just one last rhetorical question. *What else could a helpless, hopeless, once lost alcoholic soul possibly hope for? Keep at it! You have suffered for far too long!*

"No matter how unreasonable others may seem, I am responsible for not reacting negatively. Regardless of what is happening around me I will always have the prerogative, and the responsibility, of choosing what happens within me. I am the creator of my own reality. When I [review my day], I know that I must stop judging others. If I judge others, I am probably judging myself. Whoever is upsetting me most is my best teacher. I have much to learn from him or her, and in my heart, I should thank that person."

~Bill W ~

> If you change the way you look at things, the things you look at change.
>
> ~Wayne Dyer

LIFELOVEQUOTESANDSAYINGS.COM

FULFILLING THE CONDITIONS FOR RECOVERY

A question often asked and discussed throughout AA: "Is it possible to ever recover from alcoholism or is it the case we are always recovering?"

The Big Book does in fact give us a definitive answer. On the title page of our book, right under the book's title, *Alcoholics Anonymous,* it is written: "The story of how many thousands of men and women have recovered from alcoholism." At a personal level, however, we can only define ourselves as being recovered or still recovering on the basis of how we honestly perceive our own recovery at any particular moment in time. This is always a personal matter, not AA doctrine.

Let's make it perfectly clear that the frequently stated view in AA that "step one is the only step that can and should be done 100%, and the rest will take a lifetime to complete" has not proven to be true in our experience! What we do know is true, at least in our own case, is that when we have worked the first nine steps hard enough, long enough and honestly enough, we finally reach a point of awareness that we have in fact fulfilled the requirements and conditions related to the first nine steps and have cleaned up the wreckage from our past to the degree that circumstances make possible.

***Please note:** We used the word *past*, the present is always a work in progress and the future is yet to come. All of that is to be dealt with using steps ten, eleven and twelve.

Because the following realities have come to be a vital part of our lives today, we know what we say to be true. Please read carefully! What I say may already apply to you. If so you need to know about it.

*FROM STEP 1
We will know exactly what our problem really is and that we will have to humbly address it for the rest of our life.

*FROM STEP 2 & 3
We will now have a dynamic, growing, living, breathing relationship with our Higher Power that is very real and very personal to us.

*FROM STEPS 4, 5, 8 and 9
We will have cleared up the wreckage of our past to the degree possible.

*FROM STEPS 6 and 7
We will have found that vital sense of humility that demands that we must continue to grow in our recovery and pursue with a passion an ever more fulfilling relationship with our Higher Power.

When these things happen, our daily life will become filled with the conscious awareness of the presence of our Creator. We become aware of not only His grace and beauty delightfully evident in the physical world all around us but we begin to recognize and experience the many miracles (acts of synchronicity) that are constantly taking place in us, through us and around us. We are glad to address the maintenance steps 10, 11 at both set times of the day and spontaneously throughout the day when the need arises. Our embracing of step 12 will now include the compelling need to share the magnificent but totally incomprehensible grace filled story of our own recovery with anyone who may be interested.

We are now a part of life. We have a sense of purpose and usefulness. We feel fulfilled with all that is righteous. Despite the often chaotic and obviously uncontrollable humanity driven events of life constantly happening around us we know that behind this ego driven chaos, all is truly well because we have found that once impossibly elusive, "little piece of Heaven right here on earth." Are these extravagant promises? We think not. They will always materialize if we work for them.

As we travel forward in our new life we grow in the understanding that as alcoholics in recovery we now have not only recognized and addressed some of our very significant and challenging differences with the non-alcoholics but even more importantly, we have also come to understand that we are far more similar to those "normal people" than we are different. The truth is there is a common element that forever binds us all together in true filial fashion with that Universal Higher Power from which we all have our genesis. We come to see that whether we know it or not, we all have the same burning inner hunger to be consciously connected to that "Eternal Source" from which all love, goodness and wellness comes.

Never was this more clearly stated than by an alcoholic by the name of Chuck Chamberlain (deceased) who said: "I believe that **Good God** and **Love** in fact is all one thing. They are impossible to separate. Wherever we find one, we will find all three. Life will forever be incomplete without the conscious awareness of this trinity in our lives."

A life of wholeness does not depend on what we experience.
Rather, wholeness depends on how we experience our lives.
    ~Desmond Tutu~

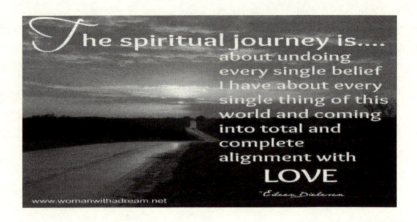

A UNIVERSAL TRUTH
(A MESSAGE OF GRACE)

One advantage of drawing nearer to the end of one's own life's journey is that we can sometimes glean from our own experience some knowledge that can possibly help smooth the road ahead somewhat for members of our own family who are in the early stages of their own passage.

A darker side of the gift of self-awareness is that we do not always *get it right*. Whether we be of addictive persona or not, old or young, man or woman, we are all subject to the down side of not *getting it right* in terms of our own sense of self or if you prefer, our ego. When this happens, we can easily lose our way. When this happens, great personal suffering often follows.

Recently, while reflecting on my own past struggles in this area and hopefully honest objective reflection, the following message came into my consciousness. Because I know these words do not originate from me, I once again gladly assign myself the preferred role of messenger and share with you what for me has become a personal and powerful universal truth.

A Grandparent's Counsel

My Precious Child

Despite how you may sometimes feel, you are not an accident.

However you may perceive it, the fact is you are the product of designed creation.

Creation does not make mistakes. You belong here. In fact, you are secure. You are valued and you are most certainly essential.

Nothing happens by accident. You must follow your heart; and then be assured that at that moment in time, as in infinite time, you are right where you need to be. You are doing precisely what needs to done, and you are exactly the individual you are supposed to be.

You are meant to live your life eagerly, happily and unafraid. You can do this because now you now know that you are never alone. My spirit is always with you.

Look inwards to discover and nurture your true strength. Look outwards to Share with others your talents your zest for life and above all, your love.

Make your love and acceptance of others your personal creed always; and peace and wellbeing will follow you for all the days of your life. Your destiny is manifest.

~Anonymous~

AFTERWORD

What follows are some thoughts that came to mind while writing this guide for which there seemed no better place to record them than here at the end of our story.

Like everything else in this book, please take it or leave it as you see fit.

As well, we want to remind you one last time that we share our experience not to change the minds of those who think differently than we do, but only to reassure those that already think as we do that they are not alone.

THE TRANSITION FROM HUMANIST TO SPIRITUALIST

This essay attempts to address the process of growth in understanding with respect to our relationship with the physical world and more importantly, our true relationship to the world of the spirit. As the Franciscan Friar Richard Rohr states, this transition involves our purposefully growing away from the more juvenile dualistic way of thinking into the more mature holistic or inclusive way of relating to the world. This can only be achieved by consistently practicing contemplative prayer and meditation.

At some point in time in our journey into recovery we will likely become aware of an insightful quote by a French Jesuit priest by the name of Pierre Teilhard de Chardin.

"We are not human beings seeking a spiritual experience; we are spiritual beings immersed in a human experience."

To just the extent we might be prepared to embrace this assumption is of course our own personal choice. For many of us, at first blush, this idea sounds great but we sense that we may have some real difficulty in embracing the concept totally. That I can understand: I experienced that dilemma for a very long time.

Early in our recovery, the best we could do with this idea was to set it out there as simply something worthy to meditate on. That is how it remained for a very long time. However, a change in our perception and ultimately our acceptance of Teilhard's assumption did however take place at some point. I suspect this change in belief had occurred slowly over time and like all growth, it was only recognizable through the 20/20 clarity of hindsight at some later point.

This change, I suspect, was probably initiated by honest but very imperfect efforts to apply the principles of positive living offered through the twelve steps. Today, the good news is that I can tell you with humility and gratitude that it is possible to be "all in" with this idea and accept without reservation the truth of the affirmation that we are in fact spiritual beings living a human experience. We can thank solely, wholly and only a loving God working through the miracle of the twelve steps for this revelation.

The more we are able to consciously surrender to this truth the more we become truly blessed with the reality that,

"God is!..... God is in us!..... God is as us!..... And God is us!..... Wherever we go He goes!..... there is no beginning and there is no end!..... Amen".

It is only at this point that we will know that we are never alone and therefore we truly have nothing whatsoever to fear about today, tomorrow and the hereafter.

Today we find it important to meditate and/or contemplate on this truth daily in order to get our head in the right place. Only then can we expect a positive outcome for the day ahead.

Please rest assured that we are not perfect in this. We remain sometimes painfully aware of our own ongoing faults and shortcomings and continue to take blessed comfort in the Big Book declaration that "we are not saints". We must always remember that our recovery is a work in progress. We just have to make sure we keep moving in the right direction. Ultimately it is only our effort that counts.

Finally, for us and we hope for you, the following quote expresses the miracle of faith at work. With unending gratitude, we discover that this priceless gift of trust and fearlessness becomes available to us due to the fact that our crushing addiction forced us into recovery which offered us access to this real faith which then becomes a most desired and necessary spiritual tool for good orderly living, one day at a time.

> "I have come to accept the feeling of not knowing where I am going. And I have trained myself to love it. Because it is only when we are suspended in mid-air with no landing in sight, that we force our wings to unravel and alas begin our flight. And as we fly, we still may not know where we are headed: But the miracle is in the unfolding of the wings. You may not know where you're going, but you know that so long as you spread your wings, the winds will carry you."
>
> ~ Joy Bell ~

THE ELEPHANT IN THE AA MEETING ROOM

To any recovering alcoholic who finds the following to be uncomfortable and may wish to disagree, we honour and defend your right to do so. If that be the case and for your own wellbeing, all that we would ask of you is to honestly ask yourself why you disagree. Because, when we know clearly why we disagree with something then we have truly learned something important about ourselves and our beliefs.

What we are about to share with you is what we have discovered in our own journeys into recovery and as the result, remains important to us to this day. We are sharing this with you for two main reasons:

First What follows, is the most important and profound truth that has ever impacted our personal existence in a positive way.

Second: Because what we are about to say is obviously a life or death matter, we are compelled to share it with anyone who may be interested.

What follows is what we have heard from a number of fellow recovering AA members. Specifically, these are individuals who began their journey into recovery by participating in one or another of the private/publicly funded treatment centres for addressing alcoholism found in virtually all major urban centers around the world today. These centres, among other things, most definitely do provide an excellent pathway into long term, healthy recovery. These treatment centers wisely send their clients back home to their communities with the strong warnings to not only find their way to AA meetings and to actively participate in the fellowship, but to make certain that they continue to actively and aggressively continue working on their personal twelve step program for long term recovery. They are told this because their personal recovery like all recovering alcoholics is a process and not a destination and will never be completed in this lifetime.

Their clients are also warned that they will come across a broad spectrum of individuals at AA meetings and to be sure to reach out to those that have something positive to share with them.

Those at AA meetings who are obviously not doing much about their own recovery other than showing up at the occasional meeting clearly have little to offer to the newcomer other than negativity. Listen quietly and choose your friends carefully. Some treatment centers even make the point more bluntly. They specifically warn their clients with the following words: *"The truth is that thousands are dying in AA clubrooms all over the world today. Don't let yourself be one of them".*

On a personal note, we who write this guide have never been inside the doors of a treatment center but from our own travels over many years inside of AA, we do sadly agree totally with this assumption. We know for a fact that the dying referred to in these clubrooms are not only figurative death but is far too often literally true as well. We are aware today that suicide among attenders of AA meetings continues to be a real and ongoing fact of life. The sad reality is that it is probably more frequent than is generally known.

One of the sad truths in too many AA meetings today is that mixed in among those individuals actively working their steps along with the hopeful newcomers, we will usually find a significant number of attendees who, for want of a better descriptor we will call passive participants in AA, or to be blunt, **the fakers or pretenders**. These are the individuals who live and often die by the adage *"Fake it until you make it"*. A quote I personally wish had never been invented. It is deadly! In a fellowship for which recovery is based on total honesty, this suggestion is totally contradictory and indefensible in my opinion. Give these pretenders a wide berth. They are nothing but trouble.

These troubled individuals fall into two categories as we see them. One group has never seriously gone near the steps on a personal level and they know it. We suspect that they have grown passably comfortable attending meetings and having memorized or stolen a few stock phrases to share at meetings so as to give the appearance of compliance with the program and to fit in. What they get out of attending meetings is beyond our comprehension. However, we do commend these folks for at least being honest with them self, if not with others.

The other group is more troubling and is the ones most likely to either experience some degree of clinical depression and sadly, to say, at least contemplate if not attempt suicide, which is the ultimate act of selfishness to those of us who have been there. These are individuals who have probably gone through one or more casual relationship with a sponsor and, unfortunately, often terminated by a personality conflict or at least expire by neglect. They have probably "dabbled" with the steps from time to time, we suspect, usually on their own, but would most likely lose interest quickly and quit. They find themselves actually staying away from drink often for many years, but continue to be burdened with a life that is none too fulfilling at best and no doubt burdened with way too much selfishness, dishonesty and fear. Listen carefully you will know these individuals when you hear them. They are the ones forever talking about their own troubles and frustrations along with the woes of the world.

We believe that members of both of these groups can be best described as those that show up at meetings day after day, week after week, month after month and in some cases, year after year simply hoping that something positive will magically happen to them. The truth is that their unrequited longing will continue until the individuals in question change their behavior or pass from the scene. We can only recommend that you stay away from these types. They have nothing positive to offer you. Frankly, they have yet to learn the true meaning of surrendering.

To those of you having read this far and are now feeling agitated, uncomfortable or pissed, we simply ask you to honestly ask yourself two questions: (1.) Is the quality of my life today meeting my expectations? And (2.), if not, what am I doing between meetings in regards to consciously practicing the principles of the 12 steps in my daily affairs?

The AA 12 step program is neither consummated nor truly practiced at AA meetings, not even step meetings. The AA program can only be accessed, applied and practiced by addressing your personal trinity at a very personal and private level between meetings. (Your personal trinity is the triad that is made up of you, your Higher Power and the life experiences you encounter moment by moment and day by day). Learning to take God with us everywhere we go is an inside job! It will take a dedicated commitment of time and attention on our part if we are to honestly expect any real results. The pioneers share that fact with us in our book when they say that

"the conscious awareness of the presence of God is the most important fact of their lives".

That my friends did not just happen to them. They really worked at it because they knew that any chance of a happy sober life depended on it. There is a real price to be paid for recovery to take place in each and every one of us. Ultimately, recovery is nothing more complicated than learning to walk with God everywhere you go. By the way, He likes your company.

THE KEY TO A FULL AND HAPPY LIFE

By this time in our journey, we can appreciate the fact that our most fundamental problem and also the source of all of our difficulties, both before and after sobriety, has been a massively disproportionate and unhealthy focus on ourselves, our plans and our perceived needs.

This selfishness drove us repeatedly into fruitless schemes and ploys to control and manipulate circumstances and people for our own misguided ends. From this knowledge, we have come to see that we were not only an abject failure at the business of living successfully but also that our extreme self centredness was in fact the *"root of our living problems both then and today."* We know this to be true whether drinking or sober and regardless of how far away from the last drink we have moved.

The 12 steps have taught us that practicing humility is not only the opposite of self-centeredness, it is, without a doubt, the only possible antidote for this otherwise deadly condition of extreme self centredness. Humility is the essential starting point for recovery from alcoholism or any other addiction and is also the key to accessing real happy, healthy living.

Because humility often seems to be very difficult to find, it can be helpful to understand that humility is 100% experiential and can never be acquired like an Idea or even a belief, it can only be experienced when we are in the right mental and spiritual condition to recognize its presence in us when it is there. That being the case, we are then left with the question of how do I consciously and pragmatically put myself into the appropriate mental and spiritual state of mind to experience this thing called humility?

THIS IS HOW WE DO IT:

Our Creator asks only that we do our best each day to turn our will and our life over to His care and protection. We do this by using the intelligence He gave us to direct our thinking and our intentions towards consciously surrendering our ego and self-will to our Higher Power.

We do this through application of the step 3 prayer. The wording of this prayer is of course quite optional, it is the intent that counts. The following simple action honestly taken is the specific action that leads us to not only the experience of true humility but more importantly the conscious awareness of living in the presence of our Heavenly Father's guidance and love. In this moment of grace we experience true humility but also honest meaningful faith and spiritual wellbeing.

Therefore we must constantly practice acceptance of the uncontrollable and embrace the task of accommodating and adjusting to reality while staying true to our values and beliefs. The call to action is no more or less than the continuing and repeated act of surrender.

SURRENDER! SURRENDER! SURRENDER!

Acceptance of the things we cannot change is the definition of the above spiritual call to action echoing throughout the twelve steps of recovery. Be aware that there is a price to be paid. That price is the giving up of our self-will. The conscious giving up of personal control of one's life is only possible if there is a real belief and trust in a God personally meaningful to us. Only at this point can we honestly claim to know the meaning of true humility.

May we all grow in understanding and effectiveness as we continue our journey of uncovering, discovering, discarding and in time, recovering.

Always remember, our thoughts are never permanent. Whether they are good or bad, the most commonly occurring thoughts are those that are repeated over and over again. The change of bad thinking into good thinking can and will occur over time with diligent practice. Over much practice and time these new positive and powerful ideas will become new fundamental beliefs or tenets entrenched in our psyche. At this point they will become our *default thoughts* that will often pop into our awareness seemingly on their own. At this point, we will reap the specific results of those default thoughts, no more, no less. Yes: It is true: Recovery is very hard work. That is, until we can discover it to be a labor of love.

Never forget that because we are not omnipotent, our view of life is always limited and therefore incomplete. However, our perception of life, regardless of how limited it may be, is all we have to work with. To assume too much can be a costly mistake. We learn, often the hard way that if we forget humility and insist on putting our personal conclusions, opinions or even beliefs about anything beyond honest self-doubt is to put ourselves into yet another untenable and potentially uncomfortable situation. To do this is to once again allow our self- will to run riot. The fact is, today, we will find all those who claim to know "truth" either in the nuthouse or wandering aimlessly somewhere out there in the weeds. They are truly the lost souls of the human race. I know this because I was once out there with them.

ACKNOWLEDGEMENTS

The following is a very short list of individuals who have played a direct and positive role in getting me to where I am today and specifically in getting this chip of a book completed. This is not meant to be a comprehensive list because my feeble memory does not permit that. I know that some individuals may well have been overlooked. To you I apologize and ask to be forgiven. Any omissions are accidental. The list is in no particular order and to those I have missed, I trust that each of you knows the role you have played and my appreciation to you for that.

~Lee Downey: My wife and best friend. How can one man be so fortunate?

~George R: My sponsor: In the beginning a necessary mentor: Today a most highly valued friend.

~Gary Q: We started our journey together and today we continue to walk the walk.

~Marcel C: A later day friend whose honesty and humility I appreciate very much. A true friend!

~Don W: His message of hope and encouragement kept me coming back.

~Lynne Hindle: My sister whose love and support means the world to me.

~Les U: A good friend from my school days. We share a common solution today.
~John Mc: A friend from Texas. He doesn't just talk "the talk", he lives it and it looks good on him.

~To my **Family** I say thank you all for being who you are and allowing me to be who I am.

~A special thank you as well to **Mary Broderick** for her interest - her unending patience and time - her publishing expertise - her advice and encouragement. Her help has been truly priceless.

~Last but not least, a special nod of gratitude to the *"Higher Power"* that can only be known personally and intimately to each of us; for the knowledge of who we really are and the grace to walk this earth with dignity, and purpose, secure in both body and soul.

Dare to Be

When a new day begins, dare to smile gratefully.

When there is darkness, dare to be the first to shine a light.

When there is injustice, dare to be the first to condemn it.

When something seems difficult, dare to do it anyway.

When life seems to beat you down, dare to fight back.

When there seems to be no hope, dare to find some.

When you're feeling tired, dare to keep going.

When times are tough, dare to be tougher.

When love hurts you, dare to love again.

When someone is hurting, dare to help them heal.

When another is lost, dare to help them find the way.

When a friend falls, dare to be the first to extend a hand.

When you cross paths with another, dare to make them smile.

When you feel great, dare to help someone else feel great too.

When the day has ended, dare to feel as you've done your best.

Dare to be the best you can –

At all times, Dare to be!

— Steve Maraboli

VeryBestQuotes.com

THE WAY IT IS

There is a thread you follow.

It goes among things that change.
But it does not change.

People wonder about what you are pursuing.
You have to explain about the thread.
But it is hard for others to see.

While you hold it you cannot get lost.

Tragedies happen; people get hurt or die; and you suffer and get old. Nothing you do can stop time's unfolding.

You don't ever let go of the thread

~William Stafford~
(Written six weeks before his death in 1998)

APPENDIX

To believe in God is a creation of the mind and is called a spiritual awakening. To know the presence of God is a product of the soul and is known as a spiritual experience. - Anonymous

The fellowship of AA is a shared reality. Recovery through the practice of the 12 steps is a totally personal matter. - Anonymous

When I am practicing my faith in all of my affairs I don't have time to feel sorry for myself. - Anonymous

When my relationship to the world around me includes the collective pronoun "we" rather than the singular "me"; I suspect I am as close to sanity (true reality) as I can possibly be. - Anonymous

Our real problem is a lack of power. Without willingly seeking access to a higher power, however we define it, we are forever doomed to being a victim to life's unrelenting slings and arrows. At best, we are destined for more disappointment, hurt and fear. - Anonymous

Life is what it is. How we interpret life is the difference. God is the perfect gentleman/lady. He / She never arrives without an invitation. - Anonymous

Pain is the touchstone of spiritual growth. Without it, we are not motivated to change. – Author Unknown

Don't allow the pride, ego and insecurities of others to stunt your growth. – Author unknown

I am never in control of what happens around me, but I am always in control of what happens within me. - Anonymous

Real success requires an ongoing commitment to the practice of personal humility, the most highly coveted and personally rewarding of all possible human qualities. - Anonymous

All people are of equal value. All opinions are not. In order to establish and maintain social order and tolerance it behooves us all to be willing and able to recognize this fact. – Author Unknown

When we come to learn and accept that we are not human beings trying to become spiritual beings but that the opposite is the true reality, we will take a giant step towards reaching our full potential. – Pierre Teilard du Chardan

Turning your attention outward instead of inward is the essential first step towards living your life as "a part of something", instead of being apart from and as the result just a lonely observer. – Author Unknown

We can only live our life through the perspective of our personal understandings and beliefs. We do ourselves a disservice if we let others persuade us without question to "see it" their way. Let us make sure that we are always true to ourselves. – Author Unknown

Hope can be a powerful force. Maybe there is no actual magic in it, but when you know what you hope for most and hold it like a light within you: You can make things happen, almost like magic. – Author Unknown

"Be impeccable with your word. Speak with integrity. Say only what you mean. Avoid using the word to speak against

yourself or to gossip about others. Use the power of your word in the direction of truth and love." – Don Miguel Ruiz

"Don't take anything personally. Nothing others do is because of you. What others say and do is a projection of their own reality, their own dream. When you are immune to the opinions and actions of others, you won't be the victim of needless suffering." – Don Miguel Ruiz

"Don't make assumptions. Find the courage to ask questions and to express what you really want. Communicate with others as clearly as you can to avoid misunderstandings, sadness and drama. With just this one agreement, you can completely transform your life." – Don Miguel Ruiz

"Always do your best. Your best is going to change from moment to moment; it will be different when you are healthy as opposed to sick. Under any circumstance, simply do your best and you will avoid self-judgment, self-abuse and regret." – Don Miguel Ruiz

"Just imagine becoming the way you used to be as a very young child, before you understood the meaning of any word, before opinions took over your mind. The real you is loving, joyful, and free. The real you is just like a flower, just like the wind, just like the ocean, just like the sun." – Don Miguel Ruiz

"When we believe in lies, we cannot see the truth, so we make thousands of assumptions and we take them as truth. One of the biggest assumptions we make is that the lies we believe are the truth!" – Don Miguel Ruiz

"We only see what we want to see; we only hear what we want to hear. Our belief system is just like a mirror that only shows us what we believe." – Don Miguel Ruiz

"The whole world can love you, but that love will not make you happy. What will make you happy is the love coming out of you." – Don Miguel Ruiz

"The more you practice gratitude, the more you see how much there is to be grateful for, and your life becomes an ongoing celebration of joy and happiness." – Don Miguel Ruiz

"You are responsible for what you say, but you are not responsible for how your words are interpreted." – Don Miguel Ruiz

"You don't need to change the world; you need to change yourself." – Don Miguel Ruiz

"If others tell us something we make assumptions, and if they don't tell us something we make assumptions to fulfill our need to know and to replace the need to communicate. Even if we hear something and we don't understand we make assumptions about what it means and then believe the assumptions. We make all sorts of assumptions because we don't have the courage to ask questions." – Don Miguel Ruiz

"If you are aware that no one else can make you happy, and that happiness is the result of love coming out of you…this is the Mastery of Love" – Don Miguel Ruiz

"Personal importance, or taking things personally, is the maximum expression of selfishness because we make the assumption that everything is about 'me'." – Don Miguel Ruiz

"You are never responsible for the actions of others; you are only responsible for you. When you truly understand this, and refuse to take things personally, you can hardly be hurt by the careless comments or actions of others." – Don Miguel Ruiz

"Nothing other people do is because of you. It is always because of them self. People live in their own dream, in their own mind; they are in a completely different world from the one we live in. When we take something personally, we make the assumption that they know what is in our world, and we try to impose our world on their world." – Don Miguel Ruiz

"If you are impeccable with your word, if you don't take anything personally, if you don't make assumptions, if you always do your best, then you are going to have a beautiful life. You are going to control your life one hundred percent." – Don Miguel Ruiz

"The way you see the world will depend upon the emotions that you are feeling. When you are angry, everything around you is wrong, nothing is right." – Don Miguel Ruiz

"The only reason you are happy is because you choose to be happy. Happiness is a choice, and so is suffering." – Don Miguel Ruiz

It's not about perfect. It's about effort. And when you bring that effort every single day, that's where transformation happens. That's how change occurs. - Anonymous

A failure is not always a mistake it may simply be the best one can do under the circumstances. The real mistake is to stop trying. – B. F. Skinner

Everything that irritates us about others can lead us to an understanding of ourselves. – Carl Jung

Where love rules, there is no will to power; and where power predominates, there love is lacking. The one is the shadow of the other. - Carl Jung

When what we demand from life does not conform to what life has to offer and our kit of spiritual tools is nowhere to be found, we are in deep trouble. - Anonymous

It's not what I know that keeps me sober it's what I do that keep me sober. – Anonymous

Spiritual awakenings are often wrapped up as rude awakenings so you better pay attention – Author Unknown

The most powerful and life altering message I have ever received came to me as a seemingly simple two word, five letter statement: God is! - Anonymous

Hope can be a powerful force. Maybe there's no actual magic in it, but when you know what you hope for most and hold it like a light within you, you can make things happen, almost like magic. – Author Unknown

Do not spoil what you already have by desiring what you have not; remember that what you now have was once among the things you only hoped for. – Author Unknown

"If you hang out with chickens, you're going to cluck and if you hang out with eagles, you're going to fly." ― Steve Maraboli

"I avoid looking forward or backward, and try to keep looking upward." – Charlotte Bronte

"The best time to plant a tree was 20 years ago. The second best time is now." – Chinese proverb

"Sometimes you can only find Heaven by slowly backing away from Hell." – Carrie Fisher

"Believe you can and you're halfway there." – Theodore Roosevelt

"Nothing is impossible; the word itself says, 'I'm possible!'" – Audrey Hepburn

"People often say that motivation doesn't last. Neither does bathing. That's why we recommend it daily." – Zig Ziglar

"What lies behind us and what lies before us are tiny matters compared to what lies within us." – Ralph Waldo Emerson

"Success is the sum of small efforts, repeated day in and day out." – Robert Collier

"It's difficult to believe in yourself because the idea of self is an artificial construction. You are, in fact, part of the glorious oneness of the universe. Everything beautiful in the world is within you." – Russell Brand

"When everything seems to be going against you, remember that the airplane takes off against the wind, not with it." – Henry Ford

"If we are facing in the right direction, all we have to do is keep on walking." – Zen proverb

"Though no one can go back and make a brand new start, anyone can start from now and make a brand new ending." – Carl Bard

"It is not easy to find happiness in ourselves, and it is not possible to find it elsewhere." – Agnes Repplier

"If things go wrong, don't go with them." – Roger Babson

"Our greatest glory is, not in never failing but in rising up every time we fail." – Ralph Waldo Emerson

"When the past calls, let it go to voicemail. Believe me; it has nothing new to say." – Unknown

"Everyone has inside of him a piece of good news. The good news is that you don't know how great you can be! How much you can love! What you can accomplish! And what your potential is!" – Anne Frank

"It always seems impossible until it's done." – Nelson Mandela

"The greatest mistake you can make in life is to continually be afraid you will make one." – Elbert Hubbard

"Tomorrow is the most important thing in life. It comes into us at midnight very clean. It's perfect when it arrives and it puts itself in our hands and it hopes we've learned something from yesterday." – John Wayne

"What progress, you ask, have I made? I have begun to be a friend to myself." – Hecato

"Every worthy act is difficult. Ascent is always difficult. Descent is easy and often slippery." – Mahatma Gandhi

"Life is like riding a bicycle. To keep your balance you must keep moving." – Albert Einstein

"Every noble work is at first impossible." – Thomas Carlyle

"The great thing in this world is not so much where you stand, as in what direction you are moving." – Oliver Wendell Holmes

"Every strike brings me closer to the next home run." – Babe Ruth

"I've been absolutely terrified every moment of my life – and I've never let it keep me from doing a single thing I wanted to do." – Georgia O'Keeffe

"Keep steadily before you the fact that all true success depends at last upon yourself." – Theodore T. Hunger

"Character cannot be developed in ease and quiet. Only through experience of trial and suffering can the soul be strengthened, ambition inspired, and success achieved." – Helen Keller

"Never say anything about yourself you do not want to come true." – Brian Tracy

"If you hear a voice within you say 'you cannot paint,' then by all means paint and that voice will be silenced." – Vincent Van Gogh

"To improve the golden moment of opportunity, and catch the good that is within our reach, is the great art of life." – Samuel Johnson

"As one goes through life, one learns that if you don't paddle your own canoe, you don't move." – Katharine Hepburn

"Happiness is where we find it, but rarely where we seek it." – J. Petit Senn

"We may think there is willpower involved, but more likely … change is due to want power. Wanting the new addiction more than the old one. Wanting the new me in preference to the person I am now." – George Sheehan

"What makes the desert beautiful is that somewhere it hides a well." – Antoine de Saint-Exupery

"Man never made any material as resilient as the human spirit." – Bernard Williams

"I dwell in possibility." – Emily Dickinson

"The only journey is the one within." – Rainer Maria Rilke

"What is addiction, really? It is a sign, a signal, and a symptom of distress. It is a language that tells us about a plight that must be understood." – Alice Miller

"If you accept the expectations of others, especially negative ones, then you never will change the outcome." – Michael Jordan

"I can't change the direction of the wind, but I can adjust my sails to always reach my destination." – Jimmy Dean

"When you get into a tight place and everything goes against you, till it seems you could not hang on a minute longer, never give up then, for that is just the place and time that the tide will turn." – Harriet Beecher Stowe

"The only person you are destined to become is the person you decide to be." – Ralph Waldo Emerson

Made in the USA
Columbia, SC
01 February 2022